A CENTURY OF STYLE: SHOES

A CENTURY OF STYLE: SHOES

ICONS OF STYLE IN THE 20TH CENTURY
ANGELA PATTISON
NIGEL CAWTHORNE

APPLE

A QUARTO BOOK

Published by Apple Press
The Old Brewery
6 Blundell Street
London N7 9BH

Copyright © 1998 Quarto Publishing plc

Reprinted 2000

ISBN 1 84092 076 9

This book was designed and produced by
Quarto Publishing plc
The Old Brewery
6 Blundell Street
London N7 9BH

Project Editors Tom Whyte, Marilyn Inglis,
Rebecca Moy
Editors Henrietta Wilkinson, Maggi McCormick,
Jennifer Baines
Editorial Director Gilly Cameron Cooper

Designer Paul Hetherington
Design Assistants Sabine Heitz, David Kemp
Assistant Art Director Penny Cobb
Picture Researcher Zoë Holtermann,
Henny Letailleur
Photographer Richard Gleed
Illustrator Judy White
Art Director Moira Clinch

Manufactured in Singapore by
Eray Scan Pte Ltd
Printed in China by Leefung-Asco
Printers Ltd

Contents

Part Two

Y008221

Introduction

Buttoned bar shoe (*above*) has delicate stitching on the vamp and a decorative heel with tiny glass and metal inlays.

Black suede evening shoe (*above*) with curved louis heel, is charmingly defcorated with tiny sequins.

Before the present century cobbling was a lowly trade, ranking alongside those of the carpenter, blacksmith, and seamstress. Designing a shoe was not thought a separate, artistic pursuit, it was just part of the whole process of making one. The rise of the celebrity shoe designer is largely a European phenomenon because America began the modern massproduced footwear industry that quickly made individual shoe craftsman redundant.

The American industry began in the colonies of New England where farmers would make the families' shoes in the kitchen during the winter months. The whole family took a hand in the work. The men would cut the leather and attach the sole, while the women bound the edges. Colonial cobblers' benches are now collectors' items.

As they had already developed shoemaking skills, some enterprising farmers set up little workshops where three or four assistants assembled, soled, and finished shoes from pieces ready stitched by the local cobbler. In 1750, a workshop opened in Lynn, Massachusetts, where this idea was taken further. Instead of each worker making up an individual shoe, each individual operation in the shoe's construction was handled by a man specifically trained for the task. The production line had started.

Initially, shoes were still bespoke (made to order), but to keep the workers busy during slack periods they made unordered shoes. Known as sale shoes, these were put on display in the windows of local shops. Two brothers named Harvey loaded a wagon with sale shoes and sold them in outlying areas. Then, in 1793 in Boston, they set up the first retail shoe store where ready-to-wear shoes could be bought on Wednesdays and Saturdays.

Inventors had been at work on developing the sewing machine since the middle of the 1700s, but the first one that was intended principally for leatherwork was developed in 1790 by an Englishman called Thomas Saint. It was little more than a vertically mounted cobbler's awl which punched a hole in the leather.

In England, Sir Marc Brunel, onetime chief engineer of New York harbor, developed a press that joined the upper of a shoe to the sole with the aid of metal pins. This was part of the British war effort against Napoleon and, with the aid of invalid soldiers, Brunel produced 400 pairs of shoes a day. But when the war ceased, the British shoe industry went back to its handcrafting ways.

A similar American machine appeared in 1810. Meanwhile, in Paris, two Frenchmen, Gengembre and Jolicière, also developed machines. Brecht of Stuttgart, a German shoemaker, experimented by using screws to join the uppers to the soles. But it was another American, Nathaniel Leonard of Merrimac, Massachusetts, who perfected the shoenailing machine in 1829.

In about 1812, Thomas Blanchard of Sutton, Massachusetts, adapted a gunstock lathe into a machine for carving lasts, the footshaped wooden blocks on which shoes are assembled. In the 1830s, again in New England, shoemakers started using patterns to aid the clipping of the uppers, rather than depending on the skill of an individual cutter. And in the 1840s, rolling machines were introduced to compress the leather to make the counters that reinforce the back of the shoe.

In 1846, Elias Howe of Spencer, Massachusetts, patented a sewing machine. Although it was designed to sew cloth, it could be adapted to sew leather with waxed thread. Three years later in Boston, the American inventor Isaac M. Singer developed his improved model with a foot treadle.

In 1858, Lyman B. Blake invented a machine for sewing the soles to the uppers. The machine was perfected two years later by a gentleman named McKay. Blake and McKay joined forces and secured a monopoly on machinemade boots and shoes for the next 21 years. The British continued to make shoes by hand until the end of the 1800s, when economic conditions forced them into machine production. They then found that all the patents

French calf-length boot (*above left*) with louis heel. Dating from the late 1800s, they display beautifully detailed workmanship in maroon satin with floral embroidery. The black and maroon, leather and silk "straights" from the U.S., c. 1830s (*above right*) could theoretically fit either foot.

Hinged wooden shoe stretcher (*below*), dating from about 1904.

Men's tie shoe with a hinged wooden sole and metal toepiece (*above left*); Belgian, 1943. Beige suede court shoe (*above right*). The sueded leather sole is unusually curved up around the upper to form a decorative edge.

were American and had to hire American machines and pay royalties for their use. But it left England with a strong tradition of handmade shoe production.

In Italy, the tradition of handmaking shoes lasted long into the 1900s, while in France custommade shoe design became closely enmeshed with the haute couture fashion house, where there was little call for mass production.

The Parisian haute couture industry had been founded by Englishman Charles Frederick Worth when he opened his store at 7, Rue de la Paix in Paris in 1858. He was the first to prepare a collection each season and have it modeled by young girls. The first man to become prominent in the world of fashion, he also pioneered the system of designing dresses that could be

Anatomy of a Shoe

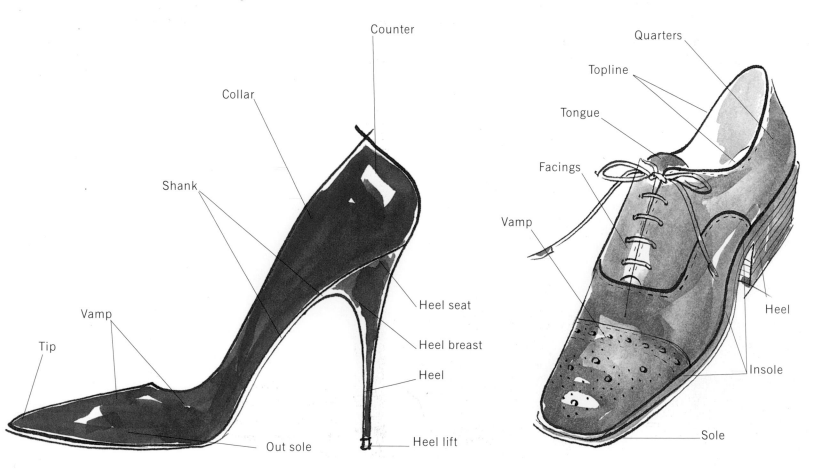

copied in the workrooms of Paris and distributed around the world. His first big opportunity came when Princess Pauline de Metternich, the wife of the Austrian ambassador to France, wore one of his dresses to a ball at the court of Napoleon III. Soon Worth was dressing the Empress Eugènie, Napoleon III's wife, and the other great ladies of the court. He created the sumptuous, crinolined gowns of the Second Empire and introduced the bustle, which became standard women's wear in the 1870s and 1880s. Worth was the great arbiter of taste and by the time of his death in 1895 he was making gowns for every royal house in Europe. Secret, unlabeled shipments were even sent to the court of Queen Victoria.

After Worth's death, the business was run by his sons, Gaston and Jean Philippe. They soon realized that fashion was changing fast and in 1900, to keep up with changing tastes, they hired the designer Paul Poiret who was then only 21 years old. Poiret's *avant-garde* designs were soon seen on the most famous figures of the time and, after four years with Worth, he left to set up on his own. By that time, a number of other haute couture houses—Paquin, Chéruit, Doucet—had sprung up around Worth's premises and the neighboring Place Vendôme, and Paris had been established as the center of world fashion.

Most shoemakers worked anonymously for the fashion houses, but a few began making their names as independent shoe designers. The same fashionable women who were dressed by Poiret or Paquin were shod by Chapelle, in Rue Richelieu, or Ferry, in Rue de la Grange Battelière.

Pinet, in the Rue Paradis Poissonière, was the most fashionable of these *bottiers*. Born in 1817, he was the son of a provincial cobbler and learned shoemaking from his father. He arrived in Paris in 1855 and rose on Worth's coat-tails, establishing a reputation among couture buyers that largely rested on the Pinet heel, which was thinner and straighter than the popular louis heel. When Pinet retired, his son took over the business. Pinet shoes were renowned for their elegance right up to the Second World War.

While Pinet's stores in London and Paris attracted thousands of customers,

Domenick DiMeola, master shoe craftsman at the firm of Johnston & Murphy (*above*).

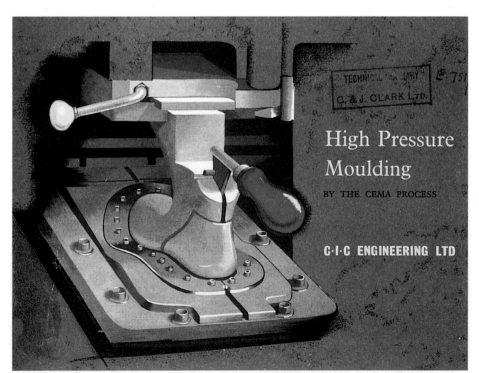

Lasting machine for a man's shoe (*left*). The leather is pulled over the foot shape which is firmly levered into place.

Satin evening shoes with crystal encrusted heel (*above*), designed by Delman especially for the singer and actress Marlene Dietrich.

another famous shoe designer, who began work in Paris during the First World War, took on just 20 customers. His name was Pietro Yanturni and he styled himself "the most expensive shoemaker in the world". This ensured him an exclusive clientèle and his shoes are now on display in the Metropolitan Museum of Art in New York.

Yanturni was followed by André Perugia, a young shoe designer from Nice who was taught the shoemaking trade by his Italian father. Perugia was brought to Paris by Poiret and worked for many of the couture houses. Two thousand of his shoes are now on display in the Musée de la Chaussure in Romans, France.

Salvatore Ferragamo, a young Italian shoemaker, took the handcrafting of women's shoes back to America when he emigrated to Boston in 1914. Disillusioned by the American method of producing shoes by machine, he moved to California where he became a propmaker, and made shoes by hand for the movies. Soon his shoes were in demand by the stars. When he returned to Italy in 1927, his celebrity clients remained loyal. In the 1930s, he developed the cork platform shoe that remained in fashion for more than a decade. After his death, an exhibition of his most notable shoes toured the world.

A young Englishman named David Evins followed Ferragamo to the West Coast in the 1940s and became the next shoemaker to the stars. He also produced collections for New York's most famous fashion designers, including Bill Blass and Oscar de la Renta. Meanwhile, in Paris, the legendary Roger Vivier went to work for Christian Dior, where he is credited with inventing the stiletto, or spike heel. His creations are also sought after by art museums around the world.

Now there is a new generation of shoe designers, both American and European, whose shoes are sought by clients and couturiers, if not yet by museums. But it is not hard to see that the more inspired creations of, say, Manolo Blahnik, Joan Halpern, Maud Frizon, Beth and Herbert Levine, Andrea Pfister, Jan Jansen, Patrick Cox, and Christian Louboutin will one day soon take their place alongside the work of their distinguished predecessors. Their shoes will be appreciated as works of art, rather than simply as coverings for the feet.

Bruno Magli pump.

Impossibly high, stiletto mules by Gucci (*below*). Such height demanded 20th-century technology to prevent the heels from snapping.

1

Court Shoes & Pumps

Court shoes are the "little black dress" of footwear, so commonplace and elegant in their simplicity that they seem to have been around forever. And, like the little black dress, modern court shoes owe their popularity to Coco Chanel. The court shoe is an enclosed shoe that grips the foot well enough to stay on of its own accord. It has no fastening—no buckles, no laces, and no zippers. Both the heel and the toes are covered, though the top of the foot is left *décolleté*, or exposed. The key design feature of the modern court shoe is the "court line". Even a slingback can be classed as a court show as long as the top line of the show follows a continuous line around the foot. Pumps are essentially the same, but usually have a lower heel.

A pair of louis-heeled pumps in royal blue with gold decoration. They were designed in Italy around 1790 by Della Bella, creating a look that would flatter women's feet for the next two centuries and beyond. A rainbow leather pump (*far right*) by Johnny More, 1997, styled with a low heel and highcut tab reminiscent of 1600s fashions.

Brocade court shoes (*above*) for evening wear. They have a rose-pink lining that picks up the colour of the rhinestone-centered rose that is set to one side. They were designed in France in the period 1912–16.

AN ARBITER OF STYLE

Court shoes originated in the Middle Ages at the 12th-century court of Queen Eleanor of Aquitaine (now part of France). The arbiter of style in her court of love was her lover, the troubadour, or love poet, Bernard de Bertand. He introduced long flowing gowns with trains in soft material. To go with these elegant gowns, women at court wore pointed shoes. It is likely that the name "court" shoes originated because they were worn at court. With their toes crammed into pointed shoes, European women's feet were constricted for the first time, but enduring the discomfort this caused was seen as a mark of religious piety.

These primitive court shoes made periodic appearances in the history of footwear. In the 1600s they turned up as a men's heeled dancing shoe, festooned with ribbons.

By the early 1800s, the ribbons had gone and men wore slip-on patent leather pumps for dancing. These were emulated by women, but by the turn of this century, women had largely abandoned these primitive court shoes in favor of laced or buttoned boots.

In 1910, as skirts grew shorter, daytime pumps with 2–2½ inch (5–6 cm) heels appeared. They were made in a variety of leathers from glacé to kid, in black or brown, and were often decorated with a pompom or a bow. From 1914, pumps were available in many colors and materials, with decorations that varied every season. The designs were influenced by the ornate styles of the 1600s and 1700s.

At the end of the First World War, skirts shortened drastically, throwing new attention on the foot.

A pair of shoes that any heavy-metal rock musician might be proud of actually date from the turn of the century and were made in St. Petersburg, Russia. No doubt worn at Imperial balls, they are highcut court shoes in fine kid with filigree metal buckles.

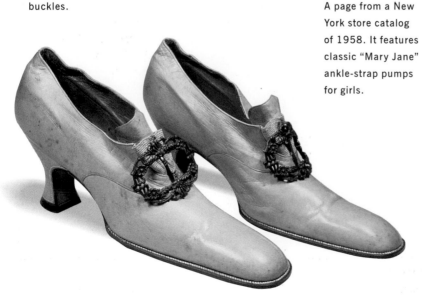

A page from a New York store catalog of 1958. It features classic "Mary Jane" ankle-strap pumps for girls.

A cream grosgrain silk pump made by Bally in 1904. It is decorated with a diamond pattern in black and crystal bugle beads around a rhinestone flower.

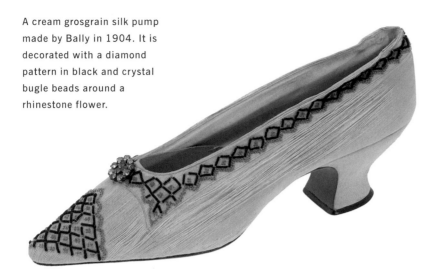

Bally court shoe of 1926 (*below*) in dark gray leather with mother-of-pearl ornament.

In 1919, the photographer Baron de Meyer created the first large feature on shoes for *Vogue* magazine. It was called "New Shoes for Cinderella," and developed the idea of the shoe as a fashion accessory.

Chanel's Elegant Influence

In the 1920s, the couturier Coco Chanel created a new type of elegance. She freed the female body from the constraints of corsets and stays. Garments were simple, soft, and unshaped. The epitome of the new simplicity was the "little black dress"—a short, unadorned cocktail dress.

Chanel liked to dress her clients from head to toe, with matching accessories. To go with her new look, she needed shoes that were similarly plain, depending solely on their simplicity for elegance. She introduced a simple, heeled, slip-on shoe, which was based on the slippers worn by Saint Ursula in a painting by Venetian Renaissance artist Carpaccio. This was the birth of the modern court shoe characterized by the continuous top line of the shoe around the foot. One exception to this general rule is the d'Orsay cut. Alfred Gabriel, Count d'Orsay, was considered to be the last of the dandies in Paris during the 1800s. He was an author, artist, and man-about-town, but

Made in 1904 by Bally in Europe, this is a louis-heeled court shoe designed to complement the elegant Edwardian gowns of the period. It is made entirely of leather, with a decorative tongue and a delicate floral pattern in gilt beads.

The Palter dynasty

The name Palter has been a fixture in the world of American footwear for three generations. The Dan Palter Shoe Company was founded in 1919. Founder Dan Palter teamed up with Jim de Liso in 1927. The company changed its name to Palter de Liso and went on to make fashion history until 1975, when it closed.

Along with Andrew Geller, Charles Miller, and Seymour Troy, Dan Palter was one of the giants of the New York fashion industry during its golden era in the 1920s, 1930s, and 1940s. In 1937, he won the prestigious Neiman Marcus Award for the introduction of platform shoes and open-toed slingbacks. These were styles that would dominate shoe fashion for the next 10 years. He also won the first Coty Fashion Award and was one of the founders of the Color Co-op, which launched colored leather in the 1930s.

Dan Palter's two sons, Dick and Buddy, both went into the shoe business. Dick took over Palter de Liso, which he ran until 1975. Then he started the Robert Gil brand, which he ran until 1992. Since then he has been working as a consultant to the industry.

Buddy left the family business in the 1940s. He was an account executive at Palazzio until 1969, when he picked up the exclusive North American agency for Bruno Magli's women's shoes. With his wife Harriet, he built the Magli brand into one of the biggest fashion names in America in the 1970s and 1980s. Their son Scott runs Bucci, a company that handles the prestigious St. John shoe line.

most of all he liked dressing up. D'Orsay cut deep "V"s in the sides of the traditional dancing pump, separating the front and back. The style was originally designed for men, but became it also became a favorite with women, and has made regular reappearances since it was popularized again in the 1920s. A more extreme variation is the opera court shoe where the sides are removed completely.

Flowers run riot in this stunning pair of silk evening pumps with a high tongue. They were made in England in the period 1920–24.

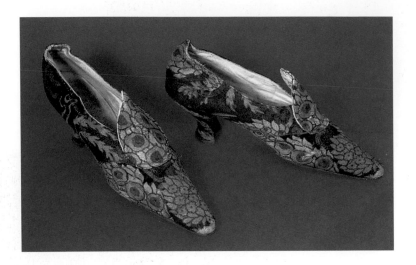

The Court of Perugia

As with everything Chanel did, others quickly followed her lead. In the 1920s, the shoemaker André Perugia, in particular, made the court shoe his own. He had just arrived from Nice and became, after Yanturni, the first of the noted shoe designers of this century. Until this time, making shoes had been regarded as a lowly occupation, and aficionados of the craft were overlooked. But after the shortening of skirts in the 1920s, shoes were suddenly on show and became as important a fashion accessory as a handbag or a hat. The new focus on footwear meant that a named shoe designer could suddenly become as famous and sought after as a celebrated milliner, or even a prominent couturier.

As a child, Perugia had been apprenticed in his father's provincial cobbler's shop in Nice. But at the age of 16, he found himself frustrated by the boring, repetitive nature of everyday shoemaking and left to set up his own shop where he could focus more of his attention on design. One of his first clients was the wife of the owner of the Negresco, a famous hotel on the seafront. Her husband let Perugia display his shoes in a cabinet in the foyer. This in turn brought him a wealthy client whose clothes came from the Paris couturier Paul Poiret.

Poiret invited Perugia to show his shoes at Maison Poiret in Paris. But it was 1914, and the First World War stopped that plan. In 1920, Perugia eventually arrived in Paris and opened a shop in the Fauborg St. Honoré in Paris. He began providing shoes, not just for Poiret, but for all the great couturiers of the time.

David Evins

David Evins has been considered "shoemaker to the stars" since the 1940s. He has worked in Hollywood and with the top fashion designers in New York. His facility to come up with some new twists on the simple court shoe has also earned him the title King of the Pumps. Although he was born in England, David Evins emigrated to the U.S. when he was 13. He studied illustration at the Pratt Institute in New York and went to work as an illustrator on a footwear magazine, which gave him the inspiration to start designing shoes.

He began to sell his designs and prototypes to several shoe manufacturers. In the early 1940s, he went into partnership with Israel Miller, one of the giants of the footwear industry, and began producing shoes under his own name. He had to keep his creativity in check while making massmarket shoes. The most popular line in women's shoes at the time was the pump, so he dedicated himself to becoming its master.

At the same time he promoted himself as a bespoke shoemaker for the rich and famous. In time, almost every woman in public life in America was shod by Evins. He was able to let his imagination have full rein. Nevertheless, he prided himself on his discipline and knowledge of traditional shoemaking, producing each bespoke shoe himself, by hand. Despite his penchant for unusual decoration, his designs are classical and the shoes well made and comfortable.

Evins first became famous in Hollywood as a result of the alligator wedge clogs he created for the flamboyant entertainer, Carmen Miranda. Later, he made shoes for Elizabeth Taylor, Lena Horne, Ava Gardner, and Grace Kelly. Not only did he make their offscreen shoes, he also dressed their feet for their greatest box office hits. He was also the favorite shoemaker of the Duchess of Windsor. David Evins has worked with top American designers Geoffrey Beene, Bill Blass and Oscar de la Renta and he made the shoes Nancy Reagan wore to her husband's inaugurations in 1980 and in 1984.

A pair of red leather court shoes (*right*) made by the English company Manfield and Sons over the years 1928–32, with flattering latticework instep and T-strap styling.

Among Perugia's customers were Pola Negri, the star of the silent movies, and Mistinguette, queen of the French vaudeville, whose legendary legs gave Perugia a marvelous opportunity to show off his shoes. He also made an entire collection of satin décolletés for the international socialite, the Duchess of Peneranda.

Perugia's star went into eclipse after World War II. But between 1962 and 1965, he teamed up with the French shoe designer Charles Jourdan. Shortly afterward, he retired and donated his priceless collection of shoes to Jourdan, who continued the Perugia tradition of producing elegant court shoes.

In the 1920s, Perugia insisted his clients wore high heels, even for dancing. The pointed high-heel shoe with a single bar strap across the instep was so widespread that is thought of as the shoe of the decade. In fact, shoes with tongues came into fashion in 1922, cutaways in 1923, and crossover straps in 1924. However, with Perugia's growing reputation, the modern court shoe came to prominence. The new liberated woman of the 1920s, it seemed, wanted to show off her feet.

Movies, Stars, and Court Shoes

The court shoe made its largest impact on the women of the world through the movies. The man responsible was Salvatore Ferragamo, who was born in Italy in 1898. Ferragamo set up in the shoemaking business in Hollywood in 1923 and made the shoes for Cecil B. de Mille's epic movie, *The Ten Commandments.*

continued on page 20

Shocking rose pink pumps (*below*) with fine silver piping and a ribbon tie. Made in England by Joseph Box, 1924–27, they were shoes to delight the "flappers" of the day with their flamboyant color and elegant lines.

Varying styles from the 1920s produced in (*from the top*) England, and Germany. Both shoes are highly decorated and are both by Bally.

Andrea Pfister

Andrea Pfister boasts that his shoes are feminine, sexy, full of humor and perfectly made. He thinks a shoe should not only be pretty but must also fit well and be comfortable. "If a beautiful woman's feet hurt, she becomes ugly," he says.

Andrea Pfister was born in 1942, in Pesaro, Italy, of Swiss parentage. He went to school in Switzerland, then studied art and languages at the University of Florence. In 1961, he entered the Ars Sutoria Institute of Footwear Design in Milan. The following year he was awarded first prize in the International Designers Contest in Amsterdam.

That same year, he moved to Paris and designed shoes for the haute couture collections of Lanvin and Jean Patou. In 1965, he presented the first collection under his own name and two years later he opened his first shop in Paris.

In 1968, he returned to Italy and began producing his own collections in a small rented factory. By 1974, he had moved into his own factory in Vigevano where, along with his own ranges, he produced shoes under the Krizia label for Mariuccia Mandelli, one of Italy's top clothes designers. At the same time he designed accessories such as bags, belts, scarves and jewelry. He opened his second shop in Paris and, in 1976, began to produce a line of ready-to-wear clothes.

His shoes are essentially Italian in the craftsmanship and attention to detail. But he brings to them a wit and irreverence. He likes to take a theme such as the sea, a starry sky, music, the circus, or Las Vegas and improvise on it. In 1975, he made a yellow pump with a cocktail-glass heel, complete with lemon wedge. Pfister called it Martini Dry. He also designed a sandal called Jazz that has a snakeskin saxophone on the upper. He loves flat shoes and very high heels, but he admits that compromises are often necessary to make shoes comfortable.

Pfister is renowned for his use of color. "Colors, materials and clear lines are very important to me," he says. Twice a year he shuts himself away for two months to created a new collection for his own label. His starting point is always color. After that, he works on shape, proportion and styling. He is color director for the Stefania tannery and devises two palettes annually

Shoes from Andrea Pfister's collection for the winter of 1978–79. He christened the design "Dandy"—one can imagine them worn with a velvet smoking jacket—and used silk-thread embroidery and soutache on faille.

Matching colors in materials as diverse as reptile and suede is often a basis for his collections. He also uses embroidery, silks, plastic and paste stones. Ornamentation is all important and his use of sequins, jewels and glitter not only added to the color of his shoes, but also bounced light around the upper and heel. He loves appliqué and covered his shoes with motifs as diverse as frogs and horses to tubes of paint. "The times are over for the decorated shoe," says Pfister ruefully. "I have cleaned up my act very much."

His clientele, which includes Elizabeth Taylor and Madonna, remains loyal though. Pfister still draws the line at making clunky, grungy shoes. "To me heavy is ugly," he says. "I never liked heavy shoes and will never do them, even if they come back in fashion, my customers don't like them." His typical customer is the woman who mixes different pieces by different designers, an

Armani top, for instance, with a Donna Karan skirt, and a jacket by Ferré. He believes that his shoes work best on a woman who's sure enough of herself to create her own combination.

His favorite design is the Birdcage shoe he created in 1979. It was an opentoed pump, with an open latticework vamp made of thin leather straps. He made it in reptile skin, which is his favorite material. It spawned millions of copies in diverse materials including plastic. But Pfister believes that imitation is the sincerest form of flattery. "The design," he says proudly, "was timeless".

Six Pfister designs (*left to right from top left*): "Comédie", the shoe that made his name in Amsterdam in 1963; "Hommage à Picasso", summer 1985; "Delft", summer 1990; "Papageno", a shoe covered in rooster feathers, winter 1982–83; "La Vie en Roses", summer 1991; and "Festival", a pump embroidered with sequins, winter 1989–90.

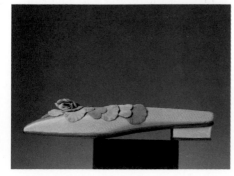

Two beautifully cut shoes (*top and bottom right*) made in the 1930s by Preciosa for Hérault in France.

A 1930s python skin, buttoned bar shoe from Italy (*top left*)—the most fashionable style of the period.
A selection of 1926 beige and taupe leather shoes (*bottom left*), in typical styles of the period including the the "J-strap", and a bow-rimmed tie. All by Preciosa for Hérault, France.

A high-fronted, straight-heeled town shoe (*above*) in fine suede with leather trimmings and a bootlace fastening. It was made by Preciosa for Hérault in 1932–36.

With the endorsement of the movie mogul, Ferragamo was contracted by Paramount to make shoes for costume dramas. He began making replicas of court shoes of the 1600s. He also had a growing reputation as shoemaker to the stars. During this period he made a critical breakthrough. He discovered that the weight of a woman's body was not carried on the heel and the ball of the foot alone, but rested on the entire arch of the foot. So Ferragamo put a thin strip of steel inside the sole of each shoe to support the arch. This spread the weight and allowed slimmer and more elegant shoes to be made.

Queen of Hollywood

The queen of Hollywood, Mary Pickford, and her sister Lottie began buying Ferragamo's shoes and another silent movie star, Lillian Gish, followed suit. For the glamorous Gloria Swanson, he created a pair of shoes with corkscrew heels, covered in pearls, stones, and gold decoration. Pola Negri ordered dozens of white décolletés, which she then dyed to match her outfits.

Soon Ferragamo was receiving so many orders that he could not fill them. Even if he stopped making shoes by hand and bought machines, there were not enough skilled operators in California to keep up with the demand. So, in 1927, he returned to Italy, settling in Florence, where he could assemble the workforce he needed. But most of his output was aimed at California.

During the 1920s, shoemakers began adding decoration to the court shoe. A simple black pump would have an ornamental crystal buckle fitted to the front of the instep. But Ferragamo, Perugia, Chanel and others realized that the plain, black velvet pump, or silver kid, highheeled court shoe remained the epitome of elegance.

In the 1930s, the borderlines between different types of shoes began to blur. Court shoes became broader, toes less pointed and heels were lowered to around 1½ inch (4 cm), although high heels remained in vogue for dancing. By 1937, court shoes were gradually eclipsed by wedge and platform shoes and sandals. But, thanks to Hollywood, the court shoe was about to make a comeback.

Hollywood Hits

After Ferragamo left California, the next shoemaker to the stars was David Evins. He is also known as the "King of Pumps". Born in England, he emigrated to the U.S. at the age of 13. He attended the Pratt Institute in New York where he studied to become a fashion illustrator. Eventually, he began designing shoes and making prototypes to sell to manufacturers. Early in the 1940s, he became a partner in the U.S. shoe manufacturer I. Miller and produced collections of classical décolleté court shoes under his own name.

It was his ticket to Hollywood. Moviem stars in the 1940s were particularly eager to show off their legs and Evins' court shoes, with their lowcut insteps, made a woman's legs seem longer. Evins made shoes for Lena Horne, Ava Gardner, Elizabeth Taylor and Grace Kelly. Kelly wore a pair of Evins' pumps at her wedding to Prince Rainier of Monaco. The pumps had low heels so that the bride did not tower over the groom.

High Heels and Lavish Decoration

Roger Vivier became the next "King of the Court Shoe." He had spent the war in the U.S., designing shoes for American manufacturer Herman B. Delman, and making fashionable hats. In 1953, he returned to France and put his considerable talents at the disposal of the French couturier Christian Dior, who had just formed the Christian Dior–Delman company. The couturier let Vivier produce shoes under his own name, a rare honor at the house of Dior.

Vivier created the stiletto at Dior, refining the high heel from the Italian sandal and

Fun shoes in riotous colors (*above*) from 1945–48 reflected the optimism after the Second World War. Made U.S. by Lamplighters, they are kitten-heeled young fashion shoes that rejoice in the name "Slicca".

Yellow lowheeled shoe of 1955 by Bruno Magli (*below*) with a large "puritan" buckle. Brown highheeled T-strap (*bottom*) of 1941 is a glamorous version of the sensible footwear seen during the war years.

Elegant, yet with a touch of Peter Pan about it, this walled, square-toed court shoe with the zigzag top line is by Hérault in France and was produced around 1932–38.

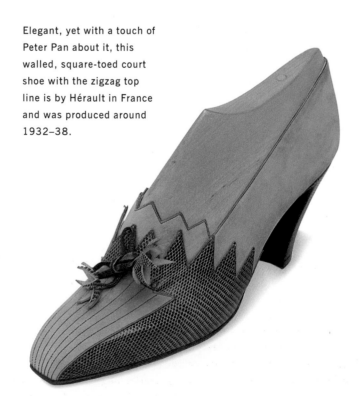

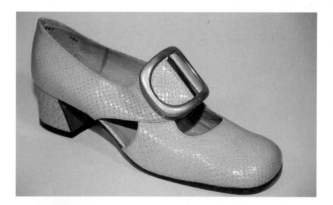

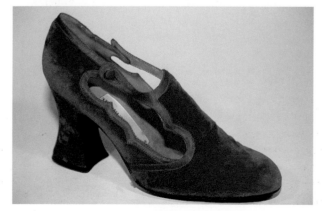

Joan & David

Joan Halpern was doing a postgraduate degree in psychology at Harvard when she met her husband David. He was the chairman of Suburban Shoe Stores, and already a big name in the shoe industry. When they married in 1968 Joan knew nothing about shoe design.

Halpern's "Chanel" pump (*above*) inspired by Coco Chanel's original twotone slingback.

Joan Halpern identified the need for a stylish shoe without fussy detail, that looked smart and would not date too quickly. Her market was the active women with a diverse and fastmoving lifestyle. She designed what she wanted, and with her husband founded the company the named Joan & David.

Her first shoes were an oxford-style tie and a lowheeled pump created to go with the pants and separates which were in fashion in the late 1960s. They became very popular indeed.

Joan learned the business at a small shoe firm in Boston and then set up in Cambridge, Massachusetts. A chain of shoe stores, franchises, and boutiques in major department stores developed, together with a range of clothes and accessories.

She learnt how to design while producing collections of women's shoes. The Joan & David label was introduced in 1977. A line of men's shoes followed five years later, and a less expensive collection, Joan & David Too, in 1987. The flagship store on New York's Madison Avenue was opened in 1985 and more followed around the world.

Halpern's shoes are unselfconscious and instantly recognizable. She makes good pumps, loafers with metal snaffles, strappy sandals, and dancing slippers with sensible heels. Colors tend to be neutral and classic, interspersed with metallics and primaries.

She designs the shoes while commuting between 38 stores worldwide, factories in Italy, and homes in the U.S., Italy, and France. Her Chinese pumps were inspired by those of a housegirl at the Mandarin Hotel where she was staying for the opening of Joan & David in Hong Kong. The company formed associations with Ann Taylor, and Calvin Klein Accessories, and diversified into purses, accessories, and ready-to-wear clothing manufactured in Italy.

In 1978, Halpern was awarded the American Fashion Critics Coty Award for Design, and in 1986 the Cutty Sark Award for men's footwear design, and was named Footwear News Designer of the Year. Among several other accolades, she was given, in 1993, the prestigious Michelangelo Award in recognition of her marriage of American design and Italian craftsmanship. The company is now based in Italy. This has lent a more European style to the shoes, but it has not divorced her from the lifestyle of her primary consumer, the busy working woman.

Joan Halpern's designs, whether court shoes, or loafers (*below*), are designed with the active modern woman in mind.

Seven shoes by Emma Hope from her "Regalia for Feet" range, designed in the early 1990s.
They are all plain, understated pumps. Six are in suede of varying colors, and one is in lace.

adding it to the court shoe, of which he was soon the undisputed master. Although he used the latest technology to produce his shoes, he drew his inspiration from the past and decorated his shoes as lavishly as anything seen in the 1700sy. The court shoe, with its plain cut, is the perfect canvas for wild and elaborate decoration. "The secret is to find the oldest forms in the world and to reinterpret them in the light of our era, with devices suggested by a different rhythm of living," he said. These devices included silk-satin uppers, pearl and bead trimmings, lacework, paste, appliqué, and jewels. The basic silhouette of his court shoes was widely copied and appeared in stores everywhere. The highheeled court shoe became obligatory at any formal event.

The Italians Strike Back

While high fashion was being made in Paris, ready-to-wear shoe production was heading south to Italy, which was in the middle of an economic boom. In 1951, Italian shoe manufacturer Giovanni Battista Giorgini's idea of holding a shoe "parade" in Florence to show off the talents of Italian shoe designers and manufacturers became a reality. The trade display immediately brought two Italian shoe designers, Capucci and Valentino, to the world's attention. Mario Valentino later made shoes for America's First Lady, Jacueline Kennedy. Creativity flourished with shoe designers such as René Caovilla, known as the "Cellini of Footwear" because of his technical refinement and stylistic subtlety, making shoes for actresses Elizabeth Taylor and Sophia Loren. Italian shoe designer Sorelle Fontana even came up with a spiked ladies' golfing pump whose heel was a tiny globe. The advent of seamless stockings without heel reinforcement brought the slingback into fashion.

Meanwhile, in Paris, Coco Chanel and her shoe designer Raymond Massaro were working in the lowheeled pump. Their new design was twotone—Chanel's trademark—in beige and black, and it had a slingback. Another Parisian couturier Givenchy followed in 1955, with a lowheeled opera pump, which was cut straight across the instep. And when Yves Saint Laurent took over at Dior in 1957, he too favored lower heels and a rounded toe that became known as the "Young Look."

The court shoe in the 1950s was almond-toed and very low cut at the sides and the top of the foot. As the decade wore on, toes began to get more pointed again, but in 1958, Dior simply cut off the point of the shoe, leaving the toe wedge shaped, although flat pumps of the time had eggpoint toes.

Heels remained low, around 1½ inch (4 cm), but decoration on the court shoe

Court shoes indeed. These black suede slingbacks (*left*) with white leather were designed by Rayne, the official shoemaker to Queen Elizabeth II of England. He created them around 1950 before the Queen came to the throne.

Salvatore Ferragamo's black patent and white leather pumps with square toes, designed in 1996.

Shoes from the 1960s (*clockwise from top right*): block-heeled pumps with a squarish toe by Pierre Gamain of Paris; white patent slingbacks by Roger Vivier for Dior; heavily embroidered pumps by Christian Dior; and Italian pumps with glass ball heels.

American-made 1960s pumps with Oriental upturned toes, a metal-look sole, and an extraordinary heel.

came back into fashion. Large bows made of chiffon, satin, or grosgrain ribbon appeared on pumps in 1957, and court shoes were given tiny straps, tabs, or crisscrossed gillie lacing to draw attention to the foot. In 1958, T-strapped courts with very low fronts came in. Broad spool heels, named after the spool of thread they resembled, came and went, though the fashion for narrow, circular heels persisted. Then, in 1959, as an alternative to the stiletto, Delamanette came up with the no-heel court shoe. Without a heel, the shoe was supported by a metal extension of the sole projecting backward under the arch and heel of the foot. The shoe worked technically, but its extraordinary design did not catch on.

Courts of the First Lady

In the early 1960s, Jacqueline Kennedy had just arrived in the White House and quickly became the queen of style. She dressed simply in tailored suits, pillbox hats, and elegant pumps, and the world followed in her footsteps. The First Lady bought her court shoes from shoemaker René Mancini in Paris, who provided shoes for couturiers Pierre Balmain, Givenchy, and Chanel. From the White House, she ordered at least 12 pairs every three months, though this dropped to eight pairs a season when she later became Mrs. Onassis. Since Jackie Kennedy, every First Lady has been seen wearing court shoes on formal occasions. Nancy Reagan's were made by David Evins.

Later in the 1960s, when skirts became shorter and legs appeared to be longer, plain, lowheeled walking pumps came into style creating the largest possible canvas for the fashionable patterned tights. Toes were pen nibbed or chiseled, and heels were less waisted. Both broadened during the decade so that, by 1970, heels were completely straight and sometimes even square. But the lowheeled pump had given way to the higher and strappier shoe with a thick sole—platforms were just around the corner.

Nevertheless, the court shoe continued to be popular. In the 1970s, Natalino Pancaldi, who ran an Italian shoe firm established by his grandfather in 1888, produced a highcut court shoe called the "Rabbi". In just over six years more than 25,000 pairs were sold from the Henry Bendel shop in New York alone.

Elastic Innovations

The court shoe was reinvented in the 1980s when designers broke away from traditional materials. Caovilla, working for designer Valentino, came up with a transparent plastic model. Both Armando Pollini and Philip Model designed stretch shoes and made the court shoe in elastic. There is some dispute as to who thought of the idea first. Pollini has registered the trademark "Elast" for the grosgrain stretch fabric he uses for his shoes. "I discovered the material in an old German firm that made corsets and bustiers," he says. "There are lots of imitations, but the quality is not the same." Model, known as Monsieur Elastique, says he got the idea from the elastic in lingerie. He also makes court shoes in conventional materials, though in jazzy patterns and polka dots.

One of the new exponents of the court shoe is Emma Hope. She trained in shoe design and technology at London's Cordwainers College. Other students have included Joseph Azagury, Christine Ahrens, Jimmy Choo, Patrick Cox and Elizabeth Stuart-Smith. Emma Hope was one of the late 1980s flowering of design talent in Britain. Her first collection went on sale in the U.K. and the U.S. in 1984 and she began making shoes for leading fashion designers Bill Gibb, John Flett, Betty Jackson, Joe Caseley-Hayford and Jean Muir.

High-heeled, platform court shoes designed by Biba, the legendary London fashion setter of the 1970s.

Three variations on a theme. These are all plain black pumps with square toes, designed by Katherine Hamnett, an internationally famous clothing designer who has been successful with her accessory ranges.

2

Slippers & Mules

Slippers are not just for the bedroom. Some of the most exquisite evening shoes of the century, made by masters, have been slippers. The perception of slippers has changed radically over the century; today, they are seen as the soft shoes worn with a bathrobe, and to wear them on any other occasion may be viewed as slovenly. But these are only bedroom slippers. In fact, any shoe made out of a soft material that slips onto the foot without fastenings is a slipper. Slides, or mules, as they are known in the U.K., are a type of slipper. They are backless, with or without a heel, with a band over the instep that holds the shoe on the foot. Slippers are not intended to be worn outdoors, but they are not confined to the bedroom. The low-heel boudoir slipper is worn as a day shoe around the house. The hostess slipper, with a higher heel, is usually backless and can be worn at home for informal entertaining. Ballet shoes are technically slippers. Men's and women's formal evening dancing shoes are often called slippers, too, but that is a hangover from the 1700s when both men and women wore slippers indoors for dancing.

An exquisite pair of American silk slippers (*above*), made in Boston in the 1760s. The Pfister mule (*far right*) is covered in hot pink felt flowers.

The embroidered cream "Empire" style slipper (*top*) was worn at the court of Napoleon I, Emperor of France, and was designed to complement the sheer dresses of the period. The English slippers (*above*) date from 1670–1710 and are in embroidered silk. Alongside them is the patten, made of wood, which was worn to protect the slippers out of doors.

TREADING SOFTLY

Some slippers, slides in particular, have escaped the confines of the house. Slides with maribou feather uppers graced the feet of Jayne Mansfield and Marilyn Monroe at premiers during the 1950s, though they have since been relegated to the mail-order catalog of Frederick's of Hollywood. Today, backless slippers with closed toes and high heels can be seen on the street, or across the floor of the boardroom, especially when they are by internationally acclaimed shoe designers such as Manolo Blahnik.

Slippers probably originated in China. They were shoes with soft, padded soles so the wearer would not disturb the silk worms that were bred in many homes. Slippers are still in widespread use in the Middle and Far East, where it is usually considered the height of rudeness to wear outdoor shoes in the house.

In the West, the slipper was the province of the rich. In the middle of the 1600s, women's slippers were made of fine satins, velvets, and silks, and were richly embroidered. Working women, who could not afford the expensive brocade fabric, could only aspire to soft leather slippers. Gentlemen also wore slippers and mules of silk and brocade at home. Most were open at the back.

Buckle Revolution

By the 18th century, the backs of the men's slippers were enclosed and they had a square domed toe and high heels. Brocade gave way to light leathers in bright colors. In the English novel of 1766, Tristram Shandy, the hero boasts of his yellow slippers. The plain finish of these leather slippers was decorated with elaborate buckles. The buckles became such an ostentatious badge of privilege that the republicans of the French Revolution raised the cry: "Down with the aristocratic shoe buckle." The Revolution resulted in the death of both the aristocrats...and the fashion. In

A pair of English slippers from the period 1710–25. High louis heels support a cut slipper in textured silk. They would have been tied with silk ribbons.

Two pairs of slippers from the early 1800s. The kid-lined, scarlet silk, be-ribboned pair (*top*) were worn by Pope Pius VII in 1811.

Birmingham, England, 20,000 bucklemakers were put out of work by the loss of their trade. But the slipper, minus buckle, continued to flourish throughout the 1800s, especially for women.

The mule, or slide, has an even longer history. The word comes from the ancient Sumerian *mulu*, meaning an indoor shoe, which was backless and heelless. The Egyptians adopted them and added a heel so that they could be worn outdoors. In the 1600s, the mule reached France, where it became known as the mulette. This backless shoe, with high heels and embroidered fabric uppers, was considered provocative footwear for both men and women.

Yanturni, Master of Luxury

Possibly the greatest exponent of the slipper began working in Paris before the First World War. His name was Pietro Yanturni. His shoes were strictly decorative and made only for very rich women. Yanturni demanded a deposit $1,000 (£625) for a single pair, in return he undertook to make a customer's shoes for life, but at his own pace. The millionairess and socialite Mrs. Rita de Acosta Lydig commissioned more than three hundred pairs of shoes from him. Her sister recalled: "You could count on the first pair being delivered in about two years. If he liked you very much, as he did Rita, you might hope to get them in a year, or if a miracle occurred, six months." Some clients waited three years for a pair of Yanturni shoes.

Yanturni was born in Calabria in 1890. He was not even a fulltime shoemaker, but was the curator of the shoe collection at the Cluny Museum in Paris. He was an authority on the shoes of every historical period, and began designing shoes because he had a passion for them.

Mrs. Lydig had a passion for shoes, too. She traveled frequently and, to transport her shoes, she

The beautiful, square-toed, green slippers (*right*) were made in Scotland around 1840–1850.

Manolo Blahnik

Manolo Blahnik has no fashion shows, he lives alone in Bath, a small Georgian city in the west of England and yet he is world famous. His name is synonymous with the most expensive luxury shoes.

Pink leather "slipper" (*above*) for special occasions, with the thinnest of ankle straps to hold the foot in place.

Kitten-heeled mule (*below*) with elegant toe and beaded decoration.

Those who dress for success call his shoes "Manolos." They adorn the feet of Madonna, Paloma Picasso, Winona Ryder, Bianca Jagger, Ivana Trump, Cher and Sarah Bernhard, and Princess Diana

Blahnik was born in 1942 in Santa Cruz in the Canary Islands. His mother was Spanish, his father Czech. One of his earliest memories is of the satin and brocade shoes his mother wore, which were made by Don Christino, the island's leading shoe-

maker. The young Blahnik studied law and literature at the University of Geneva, then moved to Paris in 1965 where he studied Renaissance art. There he saw a collection of Yanturni's shoe and they became his inspiration.

In 1970, he moved to London where his portfolio of theatrical designs were admired by photographer Cecil Beaton. Diana Vreeland of American *Vogue* was particularly impressed by his shoe designs and encouraged him to move into that field. So Blahnik began designing shoes full time. His first collection was zany. He used wetlook leather, crepe soles and chunky heels in stacked leather or shiny veneer. Purple was the season's color and Blahnik smothered his designs in cutout shapes and appliqués.

Although he has no formal training, Blahnik is a mastercraftsman. His shoes are as renowned for their comfort and the quality of their construction as their style. He is also a master of color, using vivid magenta, deep purple, bright scarlet, orange, emerald green, and saffron

Simplicity and elegance (*below*), have been hallmarks of Blahnik's designs since his establishment as shoemaker to the stylish in the 70s.

A slipper with the "weightless" quality that is a feature of many of Blahnik's designs; a single-stemmed rose is transformed into a strap along the foot (*above*).

yellow. He handles leather, suede, velvets, silks and unconventional materials with equal flair.

Blahnik opened his first shop in London in 1973. It was called Zapata, though he now trades under his own name. He also has a salon in Manhattan. From the beginning he was courted by the fashion press and he was featured in New York's *Interview* magazine as early as 1974.

The attention he receives is partly because his shoes make such good copy. Blahnik gives them evocative names such as Pompeii, Gigi, Viola, and Wisteria and their descriptions in magazines retain that theatricality: "red mules with high, knotted vamps", "jeweled satin shoes for the summer collection" and "ribbon-wrapped ankles for watered dancing shoes".

His design philosophy is that fashion should be fun. His ebullient and energetic designs reflect this. It is also said that his shoes have a weightless quality, allowing the wearer to feel as if they are floating above them.

Although Blahnik finds fashion highly diverting, he is a highly educated man and draws his inspiration from a wide field. "It could be a smell, I cannot say exactly what I

have in mind, otherwise the magic would go," he explains. He was once driving through the South of France with George, his New York partner, when he suddenly asked George to stop the car. It screeched to a halt, and a wonderful smell of mimosa mixed with jasmine wafted over the road. The perfume inspired

Blahnik to design a shoe.

One of his more fanciful ideas is to open a store in St. Petersburg, in Russia. He feels th if people could not afford to buy, they would be riveted to look. "You don't need masses of money to appreciate quality and design," he says.

Like many originators, he could have been a successful designer in another field. His distinctive sketches are highly prized, but making shoes still presents a challenge. "If I felt I had perfected my craft, I wouldn't be making shoes any more," he says.

Extraordinarily high-heeled, evening slipper (*left*) with minimum strap content.

Italian-made white leather slides from the 1950s. Decorated with birds, they have an unusual openwork metal heel, designed to resemble a birdcage complete with a bird.

had two cases made in brown Russian leather, lined in cream velvet, in St. Petersburg in 1915. One was for evening slippers; the other for day shoes. One is now in the Metropolitan Museum of Art in New York, still filled with Yanturni evening slippers on shoe trees. To keep the shoe trees light, Yanturni made them from the wood of antique violins that Mrs. Lydig bought for the purpose.

Once Yanturni had taken on a client, he took a cast of her feet. Next, he made his client walk around in bare feet so he could see where she placed her weight. He would then make shoes to fit the cast, without necessarily seeing the client again. Nor would he consult the client about the type of shoes she needed, or what they would be made of. He would comb flea markets and cloth collections to find antique materials that suggested to him a particular client's personality, he would buy the material and make it into a pair shoes, rarely informing the customer what he was doing until the shoes were finished.

For Mrs. Lydig, he used lace appliqué and silver tissue to make squareheeled slippers, with pointed or straight toes. They were the sort of slippers that might have been worn by a Renaissance princess. He particularly loved making shoes for Mrs. Lydig because, as he told her sister, "She is the only person I know who, as she walks, places her feet correctly on the ground."

No one who bought Yanturni's slippers seems to have been disappointed. His shoes were soft and light and fitted the foot so well that they felt "like a silk sock,"

Ballet Slippers

When the New York City Ballet go on a European tour, their first stop is Freed of London. Freed is the world's leading supplier of ballet slippers. The company makes 1,000 pairs a day, and top dancers get through more than 20 pairs a month.

Twenty-five individual makers work at Freed and the pointe shoes they make are so distinctive that, when a dancer finds a maker that suits her, she sticks to him for life. The tiniest variation in the paper or glue used to make the toe block can mean the difference between agony and what passes for comfort in the world of the pirouette.

Ideally, the maker will be young enough to last the dancer's entire career. When American ballerina Gelsey Kirkland returned to the stage after a two-year absence, her maker had retired and she could not find a suitable replacement. Eventually, he agreed to return and make her shoes.Makers pay great attention to detail and can remold

the lasts with plaster to take account of alterations, such as bunions, on a dancer's feet. Making a ballet slipper is relatively straightforward. One of Freed's skilled craftsmen can create a pair in ten minutes. But then the shoes have to be baked in a special oven at 140°F (60°C) for 14 hours.

When dancers get a new pair of pointe shoes, they have to break them in. They steam them over kettles, crush them in the hinges of doors and paint them with shellac varnish to harden specific patches. To customize her slippers, the Russian ballerina Anna Pavlova used almost to pull them apart and put them back together again. Margo Fonteyn used to beat hers against the stairs, while Kirkland always carries a little steel hammer to soften the toes of her shoes.

In two days of use, ballet slippers are worn out and the process begins all over again. Usually, the old slippers are thrown away, but in 1995, London's

Royal Ballet tried to cover its annual $107,000 (£67,000) shoe bill by selling used shoes autographed by the artiste to anyone contributing $50 (£30) or more. But when Rudolf Nureyev's effects went on sale at the London auction house Christies, a pair of his old shoes, which had a reserve of $50 (£30) went for $9,460 (£5,912).

according to celebrity photographer and esthete Cecil Beaton. Yanturni's designs were of incomparable elegance, and he incorporated flourish and ornament with historical resonances that perfectly flattered his clients' feet. No woman who bought from him would buy from anyone else, if they could afford it. Yanturni's services were not cheap. Outside his salon in the chic shopping area around the Place Vendôme, he had a sign that said simply: "Le bottier le plus cher du monde." (The most expensive shoemaker in the world.)

Velvets, Beads, and Jewels

For those who could not afford to be shod by Yanturni, slipper styles were hardly mundane. In 1910 *Vogue* reported that bedroom slippers were made in velvet, lace, satin, kid, suede, or brocade. They were either flat or had low, waisted Louis heels, and were decorated with ribbons, bows, pompoms, buckles, and frills.

The décolletée slipper for street wear was seen as early as 1904. This would have shocked the shoemaker to Napoleon's Josephine. When the Empress showed him a hole in her dance slipper that had developed after just one wearing, he said: "Ah, madame, I see what the problem is. You have been walking in them."

Dancing, Parties, and Coquetry

A craze for dancing begin about 1912. The tango, the Maxixe, and other risqué new dances were popular at *thé dansants*—afternoon tea dances—and evening parties. With the craze came all manner of fancy, beaded, and jeweled slippers with ribbons to tie the slippers to the ankles like ballet shoes. Women sometimes wore evening slippers made in the same fabric as the gown they were wearing. Black and bronze satin were also popular. Buckles made of cut jet, steel, marcasite, silver, gold, and aluminum sparkling with rhinestones appeared on both day and evening slippers. In

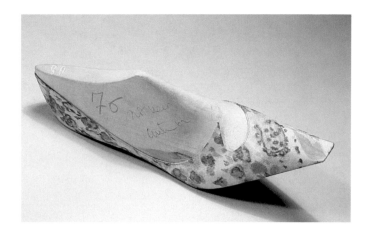

A 1962 design by Roger Vivier for Dior. This green patterned slipper has a snip toe and has been put on the wooden last to make the initial "pullover" or "model". This particular design was not used in the autumn fashion shows.

Mule with a Midas touch (*below*) on expresso soft suede with an opaque gold buckle, Joan and David.

A Seymour Troy slide (*above*), sold in the U.S. in the 1930s. It is a stylish louis-heeled shoe with a striking black and white polka dot pattern.

Made of ponyskin, this 1904 bedroom slipper (*below*) comes complete with a horseshoe-shaped silver and marquisite buckle on the two-colored bow. It was made by Bally.

"Topkapi", a precious, gold-colored kidskin babouche, re-embroidered with stras. It was designed by Andrea Pfister for his summer 1993 collection.

July 1919, *Vogue* declared: "The world is proved an ensnaring place when slippers and mules for slender bare feet droop their delicate frills or flaunt their bright ribbons with unmistakable coquetry."

The following year, chic black velvet slippers, appliquéd with geometric designs in white grosgrain ribbon appeared, heralding the new styles of the 1920s. Shoe fabrics in bright, rich colors now made a deliberate contrast with the rest of a woman's outfit. Velvets, silks, gold and silver brocades, embroidered fabrics, sequins, and beadwork were all the rage. It was a revolution in fashion, but buckles clung on. The decade began with diamanté and pearl buckles, then bronze buckles in 1922, and mirror sequins in 1924. Mother of pearl and enameled silver followed in 1925, and in 1926, they were loaded with onyx, jewelry, and diamanté. For the boudoir, red kid slides with fur edging and a high leather heel appeared.

Pointed toe slippers with fine metalized leather piping and linings. They appear to have *bal masqué* eyes on the instep, a feature that would draw anyone's attention. They were designed by Roger Vivier in the 1980s.

Sex and the Slide

The 1930s was a less frivolous decade, and the slipper fell out of favor, though the fashion designer Elsa Schiaparelli brought Turkish slippers back from a trip to Morocco, which were worn with harem pants. But by 1951, under the influence of the New Look, the foot itself was back on display, and slides stepped out onto the street for the first time. They became fashionable evening wear. In 1955, Marilyn Monroe wore a pair in *The Seven Year Itch*. The slide forced Marilyn to balance coquettishly on her toes, emphasizing her sex-kitten walk. Slides were an instant hit worldwide, eclipsing other slipper styles that had made something of a comeback

the year before. In 1954, there had been a craze for the Oriental and Turkish slippers made an appearance. But by 1955 they were dead, trampled underfoot by Hollywood's slide stampede.

In the 1960s, the low-heel slide made an appearance in paisley patterns, and there was an abortive attempt to reintroduce a slide with a high, stilted chopine sole, which had not been seen since the 16th century. In the 1970s, the slide raised its profile, appearing with platform soles, and wedges. In the U.S., Candie's slide shot to footwear fame, selling over 14 million pairs in the late 1970s and early 1980s.

The slipper and high-heel slide then tottered off to the bedroom where they remained until the early 1990s, when they were revived by Manolo Blahnik, Donna Karan, Jimmy Choo, Roger Vivier, Emma Hope, and Patrick Cox. Blahnik and Karen made them in gold; Choo in silver. Hope and Vivier settled for suede, while Cox produced shoes with the back cut off. But they all created styles wiith high heels and plain surfaces.

In 1997, the American company, Candie, brought its 1970s slide back onto the market. Fashion editors and stylists discovered that this 1970s icon had the perfect retro image to wear with the hiphuggers, leisure suits, and tube tops that suddenly filled the magazines. It also fitted in with the trend for opentoed shoes. The slide was back in vogue, and the only update in its image was that, instead of the tan and mocha of 1978, it was now appearing in yellow, orange, red, and other bright colors. The chain stores soon followed where the fashion gurus led. Some saw the return of the slide as the inevitable backlash against the sneaker. After all, the one thing you cannot do in slides is jog.

Jazzy black and white patent slides, designed by Herbert Levine in the 1960s. They are open-toed and low-heeled.

Open-toed, black patent leather slides by Bally. This high-heeled, wet-look design with gilt trims is from the 1970s.

The "Marabou" slipper (*above*), worn in the most glamorous boudoirs.

Cinderella's Revenge

Cinderella may have worn glass slippers to the ball, but they were nothing like those produced by the Italian artist Samuele Mazza. He has produced slippers made from mirrors and pieces of champagne bottles. They are part of his line of ridiculous and outlandish shoes that are designed to be art objects rather than wearable fashion. These include platform-soled shoes made to look like a baby's crib, shoes with soles that looked like staircases, and sandals made from what appear to be burning cigarettes.

3

Evening Shoes

From tango to salsa, from the ballroom to the disco, evening shoes have danced their way through the century and never missed a step. Evening shoes are party shoes and are designed for dancing. The most talented shoe designers of the century, including Salvatore Ferragamo, André Perugia, Roger Vivier, and Manolo Blahnik, have all created exciting evening shoes. Women came dancing into the new century wearing the Gaiety Girl boots that can-can dancers wore. These boots evolved from skating boots and could be stylish, with panels of gold and laminated leather. Highcut boots, which were *de rigueur* in 1900, persisted until the 1920s. But as hems soared relentlessly upward, shoes took over from boots. In 1911, *Vogue* showed a pair of highcut black satin shoes, designed for evening wear. The new century was certainly not ready for décolletée shoes. Naked ankles were one thing; naked feet quite another. As lowcut shoes came into fashion, grosgrain ribbon was crossed over the bare instep. The style came from the U.S., and stylish American women tucked a photograph of their lover under the grosgrain.

Satin court shoes in sugar pink with bow trim, complete with their original box from maker Hellstern & Sons of 23 Place Vendôme, Paris. Made in 1910, they are demure, and come under the "attractive but sensible" label, in complete contrast to the raunchy, wine red, foot-displaying number (*far right*).

A HEIGHT OF FRIVOLITY

By 1912, fashion magazines in France were talking of jeweled evening shoes with crystal and gold heels. These were superseded by heels made of jade. For those who could not quite afford such extravagance, there were shoes in satin, silk, velvet, and kid, decorated with buckles, bows, or tiny roses.

Fashion in France was influenced by art and the ideas of Futurism, outlined by Italian author Emilio Marinetti in his Futurist Manifesto in 1909, were beginning to have an impact. He envisioned a new type of women, freed by technology, who would be an agent of change in the 20th century. He also had futurist ideas on fashion: "...zigzag décolletées, sleeves that are different from each other, shoes of different colors, shapes and heights..."

These ideas resulted in evening shoes that used a mixture of fabrics and styles. They might be half tartan taffeta and half black velvet, or black leather with gilt heels, decorated with colored lozenges. However, these bold new designs symbolized a brash optimism that was about to be swept away by the grim reality of World War I. While millions of men were being slaughtered on the Western Front, evening shoes seemed the height of frivolity and they became more somber: black kid, velvet, or suede evening shoes were required wearing, though colored evening shoes did creep in towards the end of the war.

Louis-heeled, leather evening shoes in black and gold, with an ankle strap and button fastening. This eyecatching pair was made in Holland in the early 1920s.

A T-strap evening shoe in interwoven silver, gold, black and red leather, with silver leather edgings and a strasse buckle. It was made by Bally in 1928.

White leather evening shoes by Cammeyer of New York. Dating from 1908, they are reminiscent of the boots of the previous century in the way they enclose the foot and have four buttoned straps. They are encrusted with tiny beads, pearls, and rhinestones.

and with it came the tango. Hemlines rose to 8 inches (20 cm) from the floor, and heels soared to 3 inches (6.5 cm). Ankle straps became a necessity to hold the shoes in place while doing the fast new dance. Evening shoes were colorful again and made in brocade, heavy silk crepe, or silk satin, often with a metal or jeweled buckle, and set off against black lace stockings. The American dancer, Isadora Duncan, took the world by storm, urging people to throw off their shoes to dance. The fashionable resolutely refused to do so, spending even more money on handmade shoes.

Although high heels were favored by the sophisticated, flat or lowheeled evening shoes were popular during the 1920s for dancing the Charleston or the Black Bottom. Louis heels were in vogue, and so were heels decorated with stone and glass to match the buckles. Hellstern heels, named after a 19th-century Parisian shoemaker, and introduced by Greco, a 20th-century one, looked back to the 1600s. They were corkscrew heels, wider at the base than the top, decorated with beads, pearls, and feathers.

A pink, black, and gold silk brocade shoe (*above*) with a covered louis heel, and a crossover strap secured by a button fastening. The piped edges and strap are in gold leather. Swiss make, 1920.

Flirting with Fashions

Silver and gold kid were popular for the body of the shoe, along with various colored fabrics such as crepe de chine, satin, velvet, and shot lamé. Discerning women often preferred a pair of simple black satin décolletées, although more commonly dancing shoes had to be held in place by T- or ankle straps.

Fashions changed rapidly during the 1920s, and for the fashionable there was no question of wearing the same shoes two seasons running. In the early 1920s, there was a brief flirtation with all things ancient, and "fast" women wore orientally inspired, richly colored and

continued page 99

An evening shoe (*right*) in bronze satin, heavily decorated with gold and bronze bugle beads. The rosette over the instep is edged with lace, and is held in place by gold leather straps. This is a Swiss design, dating from 1924.

A 1950–51 design by Jourdan. This very highheeled, satin court shoe has a "needle" toe and a high tab front with cutout detail.

Charles Jourdan

Charles Jourdan is the biggest name in French, luxury ready-to-wear shoes. The company was established during the First World War in Romans, a small town in France. It has grown into an international corporation, marketing its name as successfully as the major Paris couture houses.

A 1934–35 design. This court shoe in deep plum suede has a low cut vamp and unusual, highcut ankle detail.

Charles Jourdan was born in 1883. He trained as a shoemaker, and at the age of 34, was foreman at a leathercutters' workshop. He was determined to branch out on his own and set up his own workshop. For two years he made shoes in the evenings. By 1919, the First World War was over, money and materials were readily available, and Jourdan enough clients to give up his daytime job. By 1921, he had a work force of 30 and moved into a factory on Boulevard Voltaire in his hometown.

Jourdan avoided the changing world of Parisian haute couture and concentrated on making solid de luxe shoes for affluent provincials. He built up an army of commercial travelers who distributed his handcrafted shoes throughout France, and backed their efforts with nationwide advertising. Jourdan reacted to the Wall Street Crash by producing cheaper lines and distributing them through chain stores. By 1939, he was employing 300 people and producing 400 pairs of shoes a day.

During the Second World War, Jourdan made shoes in felt, raffia, rubber, wood, and cardboard. Though his staff was cut to 150, he still managed to maintain an output of 300 pairs of shoes a day. Jourdan's three sons, René, Charles, and Roland, joined the firm in 1947, and by 1948 output increased to 900 pairs a day. Jourdan took a back seat, though he continued to go to the factory and work the same hours as his employees until he died in 1976 at the age of 93.

In 1950, the company began selling shoes in the U.K. Two years later, they set up a sales office in New York's Empire State Building. They were soon exporting between10 and 12 thousand shoes a season to the U.S. In 1957, Jourdan opened a boutique in Paris. It was such a success that lines formed outside. The waiting customers had to be handed numbers so they could be called when the next sales assistant was free, and Brigitte Bardot had to enter through a back door when she want to buy shoes.

The Charles Jourdan boutique was unique. It carried only a very limited range of styles and only one style at a time appeared in the window, which was changed every two days.However, every style was available in every size, three width fittings, and 20 different colors. If a woman needed a shoe in a particular color to match her outfit, she was certain to find it at Jourdan.

Similar Jourdan boutiques were opened in London and Munich. At the same time, a deal was negotiated with Maison Dior and the company began to create, manufacture, and distribute Dior shoes worldwide. In 1968, the name Charles Jourdan was franchised for the first time and he opened a store on New York's Fifth Avenue.

In 1971, the U.S. shoe giant Genesco bought a share of the company, It expanded further in Lebanon and the Far East, and began a line of womenswear. Menswear followed eight years later. The company was sold to a Swiss conglomerate in 1981 and continued to expand, opening stores in Dallas, New Orleans, Boston, and Washington, D.C.

The Charles Jourdan Group now has headquarters at 28, Avenue de New York, Paris, facing the Eiffel Tower. Since 1985, it has run the Charles

Jourdan Foundation for Graphic Design and Visual Arts and has a shoe museum containing more than 2,000 shoes made by the legendary shoe designer André Perugia, who worked with the company from 1962 to 1965. Its factory is still at Boulevard Voltaire in Romans, and the city fathers have now named a street after the town's most famous son.

Elegant high-heeled evening shoes in grey suede with piping, heel, and ankle strap in silver. Jourdan designed these in 1978.

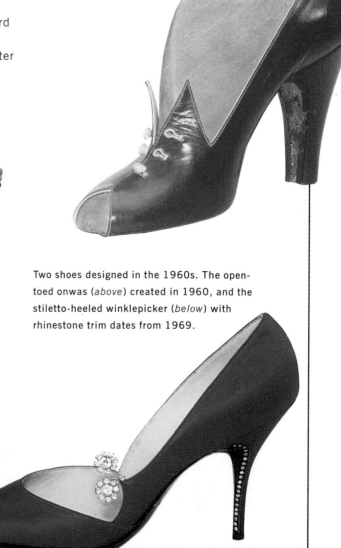

Two very open shoes, designed 21 years apart. The evening sandal (*right*) is from 1936–37. The sculptural slingback pump (*below*) was designed in 1957–58, and has an unusual ankle and heel treatment.

Two shoes designed in the 1960s. The open-toed onwas (*above*) created in 1960, and the stiletto-heeled winklepicker (*below*) with rhinestone trim dates from 1969.

embroidered harem slippers and slides. The Paris Exhibition of Decorative Arts launched the Art Deco style in 1925, and in 1926 brightly colored Art Deco shoes were all the rage.

Gold kid came into fashion in 1922, but by 1927 it had been replaced by *argenté* (silvered) kid. Around this time, experiments were made to create new types of soft leather. The first crocodile and lizard shoes were not soft enough to be worn comfortably, but by the late 1920s and early 1930s, techniques had improved and they began to become popular. Perugia, for example, combined natural lizard with patent leather. French toes came into fashion, and to balance these cutoff toes, high heels were added. The great Ferragamo then launched a high-heel sandal for evening wear.

Sobering Up

In 1929, Wall Street crashed and took hemlines with it. Subtler effects such as woven straw, pearlized leather, and crepe de chine took over. As the full horror of the Great Depression became apparent, evening shoes became sober and black. Any hint of showy silver or gold was thought to be in bad taste. "The only applied ornament which is now bon ton is that which is almost imperceptible," said French Vogue in 1930.

Chanel lifted the gloom by adding beige to the palette, and her distinctive two

An evening shoe in printed leather with a rhinestone decorated tie and a flower button fastening. It was created by Charles Jourdan in 1936–37.

A glamorous evening shoe (*left*) in apricot satin with embroidered spots. Around the instep and the heel are thin leather straps in gold, fastened with a button. The shoe was produced in Switzerland in 1930.

A gold leather evening sandal (*above*) with highly decorative padded fans in a shell motif. These wrap the foot and are joined by a bow. The shoe has a peep toe and a wide slingback, and was produced in 1939 by the Swiss company, Bally.

This evening shoe (top left) falls in the category "great to look at but hell to wear". It is a beautiful T-strap shoe with strips of crystal and looped patterned borders. The heel too is decorated. The shoe was created in the 1930s. The ankle-strapped shoe (*below left*) is from 1934, and has a bronze heel and vamp overlaid with silver leather strips.

Elsa Schiaparelli

Schiaparelli was one of the great influences on fashion in the 1930s. She was born in Rome in 1890, after studying philosophy, she moved to the U.S. where she wrote film scripts and worked as a translator. In 1920, she settled in Paris where she dabbled in writing, sculpture and knitwear design. One of her knitwear designs was seen by a fashion buyer for an American department store who ordered 40, and the House of Schiaparelli was born.

tones were born. Black remained popular, though it was gradually piped with gold or silver for evening wear. Then, in 1936, the couturier Elsa Schiaparelli broke free. Under the influence of surrealism, she let Perugia have his head. He produced evening shoes with twisted metal heels, fish shapes, or golden globes. Schiaparelli even produced yellow bootees with gold toenails painted on them and, in collaboration with Salvador Dalì, the famous Shoe Hat. Italian women took to wearing shoes by the designer Bentivegna. His evening shoes were black, long, and slender, and had high heels and buckles made of metal, or jeweled.

The Second World War hampered further development of the evening shoe. Women danced in the same wedges and platforms they wore during the day, but with the 1950s came the Italian sandal and the stiletto heel. Shoes became arched, sophisticated, and erotic. They were cut away to reveal the maximum amount of the foot, which was perched high on delicate heels.

Low-heeled silver pumps with rhinestone encrusted heels. The unusual rosettes are of tubular glass beads, threaded with gold wire and topped with silver crystal heads.

Two of Vivier's infamous needle toe shoes, with a sweeping wall on one side. He created them in 1963 for Rayne/Dior.

Roger Vivier

Roger Vivier is generally acknowledged as the most innovative shoe designer of the century. He pioneered the platform and the stiletto. His shoes have been sought by the most prestigious people of the century and are now in museums on both sides of the Atlantic.

Vivier, who was born in Paris in 1913, was studying sculpture at the École des Beaux-Arts in Paris when a wealthy industrialist friend asked him to make a pair of exceptional shoes. He was thrilled at the possibility of bringing the sensibilities of fine art to shoe making, quit college and took an apprenticeship in a shoe factory.

In the 1930s, he began his long association with American shoe manufacturer Herman B. Delman, who made up Vivier's shoes for him. But Delman rejected Vivier's design for an orthopedic-style, corksoled platform shoe. However, Elsa Schiaparelli, always fond of the extremes of fashion, included Vivier's platforms in her 1938 collection.

When the Germans occupied Paris in 1940, Vivier fled to New York, where he worked closely with Delman. But he found the shortage of materials frustrating and turned to millinery. In partnership with

Suzanne Remi, he opened a hat shop on Madison Avenue called Suzanne and Roger.

After the war, he returned to Paris to work with Christian Dior, whose New Look demanded a new style of shoe. Vivier did not disappoint. During their 10-year association, he created a number of new heel shapes for Dior, including the stiletto and the comma. He was one of the first shoe designers to use clear plastic and presented entire collections of plastic shoes in the 1940s.

He made the gold kidskin shoes studded with rubies which Queen Elizabeth II wore for her coronation. Marlene Dietrich and the Duchess of Windsor were customers. He made a celebrated pair of red faux snakeskin boots for a lifelong customer, Diana Vreeland, the editor of *Vogue*, and reintroduced the thigh high *cuissarde* boot in the mid 60s.

His shoes are on display at the Costume Institute of the Metropolitan Museum of Art in New York, the Victoria and Albert Museum in London, and the Musée du Costume et de la Mode at the Louvre.

Vivier's famous comma heel on narrow-walled court shoes with a tiny squared toe. They were part of his 1963–64 collection.

Following Christian Dior's "New Look" in 1947, the stiletto was attached to elegant lowcut décolletées, which were held in place by a little ankle strap or crossed thongs. During the 1950s, Vivier came into his own, producing some of his most memorable fairytale party shoes, covered in rich fabrics and studded with jewels. By the end of the decade, evening shoes became less constricting. The almond toe replaced the point, and court shoes were cut low. Perugia made court shoes without rigid reinforcement, which allowed movement without losing shape.

Branching Out

In the 1960s, the American designer Ken Scott, who worked in Milan, went crazy with color, making T-strap evening shoes in sparkling Lurex, and multicolored courts. When the miniskirt became fashionable, calf-length boots came in for evening wear. They were necessary to break the long line of the leg, but thigh boots were worn with hot pants.

At Dior, Vivier made silk-satin knee boots, outlined in jewels, and thigh-high evening boots in a black, elasticized knit with sprigs of silver Lurex, beads, and jet. Linen boots were studded and embroidered in silver and gold and covered with stones.

With the informality of the 1960s and 1970s, the concept of the evening shoe was eroded. It was possible to wear any sort of shoe in the evening, so the Indian sandal had its day and wedges and absurdly high platform boots were seen on the dance floor, alongside bejeweled slippers. But the décolletée was still popular because women's feet were getting bigger, and the décolletée flattered the large foot. The

Rhinestone decorated court shoes with a black lining. They were designed by Herbert Levine in 1952 and sold through Saks Fifth Avenue in New York.

White satin evening sandals (*below*) created by Herbet Levine in 1958, and sold in the U.S. They have an unusual "fish mouth", peep toe, and a jeweled stripe across the toes.

Silver snakeskin shoes sold through Simpson Sears in Toronto, Canada from 1969–71. They have a high tab front and two straps with buckles, above broad toes and chunky heels that are soled with black rubber.

Ken Scott

Ken Scott, from Fort Wayne, Indiana, became one of the most influential fashion figures of the 1960s. He studied at the Parsons School of Design in New York, then went to Guatemala to paint. He moved to Europe and, at the end of the 1950s, he opened a salon in Milan. Scott quickly became known for his adventurous use of color and was famous for his printed scarves. In the 1960s, he employed his flair for color in his shoes, using Lurex in court shoes, and reds, greens, oranges, and black together in one evening shoe.

1980s brought the craze for the designer label, and the designer shoe with it. Manolo Blahnik in England, and Robert Clergerie and Maud Frizon in France, came to the fore. Evening shoes again became encrusted with embroidery, gold, jewels, and mother of pearl.

New Wave of Designers

In America, Harvard psychology graduate Joan Halpern met her husband, David, who was chairman of Suburban Shoe Stores, and began designing shoes that sold under the name Joan and David. Nancy Reagan took up David Evins, who was creating shoes for clothes designers Oscar de la Renta and Bill Blass. In Italy, Andrea Pfister began decorating antique shoes, dipping kid in gold and pushing the use of color to its limits. His clients included Monica Vitti, Valentina Cortese, Candice Bergen, and Elizabeth Taylor.

Jeweled shoes were produced by Luigino Rossi for Manuel Ungaro, Hugo de Givenchy, and Yves Saint Laurent, while René Caovilla, son of the founder of the Italian shoe empire, made them for Valentino. Caovilla is still seen as a leading artist of the evening shoe, producing collections of embroidered, inlaid shoes, encrusted with jewels, raised on slender heels.

In the 1990s, Yves Saint Laurent showed snakeskin evening sandals, and couturier Christian Lacroix brought back the jeweled evening boot in black satin, with multicolored bead patterns, inlaid with gold and pearl. Broad, fishtail heels studded with brilliants made an a brief appearance. The shoes were silk, colored with the subtlest tints of pink or violet in wavy patterns. Décolletées in glossy velvet decorated

Black suede platform evening shoes (*below*), trimmed with python skin with matching bag. A Canadian design from 1944–52.

Sungold satin evening shoes with rhinestone decoration. They have thin, looped crossover straps, slim high heels and open toes, and were sold by London company Rayne in the late 1950s.

These would be unremarkable black court shoes but for their silver filigree wedge heels. They were created by one of the lesser known companies, Holmes of Norwich, England in the 1950s.

René Mancini

René Mancini began in 1936 with the simple idea of making dream shoes. He eventually became shoe designer to the rich and famous in the 1950s, after haute couturier Pierre Balmain discovered him. Balmain was so impressed by the shoes he saw in the window of Mancini's shop in Paris that he went in and bought 30 pairs for his next collection. Chanel and Givenchy followed swiftly and bought shoes from Mancini. Among his clients were Greta Garbo, Princess Grace of Monaco, and Jacqueline Onassis.

with pearl, jewels, and feathers also strutted down the catwalk.

Frizon does not draw her designs, nor does she cut leather. She creates them directly with the craftsmen in the Italian factory that makes them. This has given her a feel for the shoes' architecture and scope for flair and wit. At the factory, Frizon produces more than 250,000 shoes a year, and whole collections are bought by designers such as Claude Montana, Sonia Rykiel, and Azzedine Alaïa.

During the 1930s, Schiaparelli employed the artists Jean Cocteau and Salvador Dali, and was much influenced by surrealism. She made extraordinary hats, including the Ice-cream Cone and the famous Shoe Hat. Her clothes and prints were daring and unusual—a coat that looked like a chest of drawers, an organdy dress printed with huge lobsters. She used crazy, oversized buttons shaped like bumblebees, peanuts, lollipops, guitars, and feathers. Her handbags were shaped like

A white satin court shoe (*below*) with a fringe effect decoration of clear, silver and gray glass beads. A 1990 design by Rossimoda.

Ruby-red satin pumps with slingbacks that are fastened with a rhinestone and metal buckle. They were created by French-American designer Delecta in 1955.

Highheeled evening sandal (*right*) by Charles Jourdan, 1978. It is made of leather with a high, double ankle strap finished with a bow.

An elegant highheeled shoe (*left*) to show off an elegant foot to advantage. It is in shiny black leather with a beige lining, and has two instep hoops and a matching ankle strap with a simple buckle. It was designed by Joan & David.

T-strap evening shoe (*right*) designed by Joan & David, with a leather buckle, chunky high heel, and platform sole. The toe is in hand-plaited russet calfskin.

Jimmy Choo

Jimmy Choo always had his eye on America. In the early, 1980s he left his native Malaysia and headed first to London, where he studied at the Cordwainers College. Graduating in 1989, he set up a workshop in a disused Victorian hospital in London and started making shoes for Princess Diana and designers Bruce Oldfield, Jasper Conran, Anouska Hempel, and Marc Bohan. The following year, Bergdorf Goodman began stocking his shoes and, by 1992, they were available at Galaries Layfette in the Trump Tower, New York. Now he has his own store in London's Knightsbridge and his shoes are available through Saks Fifth Avenue.

An elegant pair of high-heeled pumps, designed by Jimmy Choo in 1997. The toes are of gray mesh and purple suede, with a satin rose trim. The heels are in black satin and patent leather.

balloons, or lit up or played tunes when opened. Cocteau made jewelry for Schiaparelli, including necklaces with ceramic vegetables, or metallic insects encased in clear plastic that appeared to be crawling around the wearer's neck.

Schiaparelli did not design shoes herself, but as in so many areas, she encouraged other talent, especially at the most outrageous extremes of fashion. When Vivier's platform shoes were labeled crazy by Herman Delman, Schiaparelli included them in her 1939 collection. She also encouraged Perugia in his most colorful creations. He made leopard and monkey fur boots for her, and stretch shoes made from strips of suede with elastic pieces that did away with buckles or buttons.

During the 1930s, Schiaparelli employed more than 2,000 people. But when the Second World War broke out, she escaped to the U.S., eventually opening a salon in New York in 1949. A great innovator, she died in 1973 in Paris.

4

Stilettos

High heels have been worn for centuries, but none are as elegant or sexy as stilettos. When they were invented in the mid-1950s, they inflamed passion in both men and women and ruined a million woodblock floors. The stiletto is a tall, thin, spike heel. The technology that permitted its construction was only introduced during this century. The word *"stiletto"* is the Italian for a knife with a narrow blade which was much favored by Renaissance assassins. The term "stiletto heel" first came into use in Italy in 1953. But the even thinner version we now know as the stiletto heel did not come into fashion until two years later. In 1955, the shoe designer Roger Vivier, who was working with the French couturier Christian Dior, introduced the controversial *talon aguille* and the *talon choc* : the "needle heel" and the "shock heel."

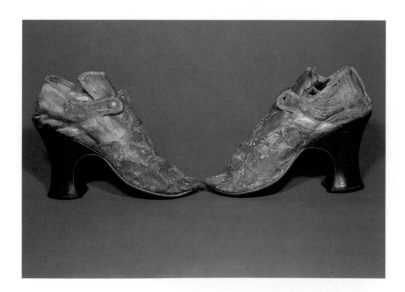

Before true stiletto heels were introduced in the 1950s there were sturdy louis heels made of leather and wood (*above*). Pfister leopardskin-patterned stiletto (*far right*).

The heights to which some women went. The three shoes above are Venetian chopines from the 1500s. They were worn by aristocratic ladies as they made the short step between gondola and palace in this city of canals. The chopine kept the feet out of puddles, was beautifully decorated and was one of the forerunners of modern-day stilleto.

HIGH-HEEL CHALLENGE

The *talon aguille* (or eagle's claw) has the shape of the classic stiletto: a broad base supports the heel that tapers from the back and the arch of the shoe, then flares again slightly at floor level. The talon choc took the art of engineering even further: the heel arches forward so the inner face of the heel is an arc, while the outer face is almost straight, extending diagonally from the back of the shoe. These styles were made possible by a steel pin encased in the heel of the shoe, which carried the wearer's weight. The same method of construction is used today.

Although the stiletto heel is a relatively new design, the search for the perfect high heel has been going on for centuries. The stiletto's earliest forerunners were discovered in a tomb in Thebes in ancient Egypt and date back to 1,000 B.C. They probably gave the wearer considerable social status, as to be tall indicated health and affluence. This idea was certainly prevalent in ancient Greece. The first great Greek dramatist Aeschylus used to mount his actors on platform shoes to indicate the social status of their character: the higher the class, the higher the shoes. Height and status were also entwined in the East. When Emperor Hirohito, the emperor of Japan, was crowned 1926, he wore *gétas*, or platform shoes, 12 inches. (30cm) high.

High heels were also associated with sex. For centuries, raised clogs 6-12 inches. (15-30cm) high were worn by Japanese courtesans as a badge of their calling. Chinese concubines adopted similar styles, and Turkish odalisques wore raised sandals in the harem, probably to prevent them from fleeing. Historians think that prostitutes in ancient Rome distinguished themselves from other women by wearing high heels.

The modern European fashion for elevated shoes came from an Italian style known as the chapiney, or chopine. Shoes were mounted on a tall cylinder usually 6-18 inches. (15-42cm) high, though at the height of the fashion, chopines rose to 30 inches. (75cm) and women had to walk supported by two handmaidens. The chopine often had a wedged sole, so that the heel was raised above the toe. In 1430, a law was passed in Venice banning the chopine, but nothing could prevent the spread of

Venetian chopines of the 1500s for aristocratic ladies (*left*) rose to a staggering 22 inches (55 cm).

A picture entitled "First steps", by artist Allen Jones. He produced many works in the 1960s that reflected his obsession with silk stockings, long legs and stiletto heels.

the fashion. The 17th-century English dramatist Ben Jonson describes one of his characters "treading on cork stilts at a prisoner's pace." And in Hamlet, Shakespeare wrote: "Your ladyship was nearer to heaven than when I saw you last, by the height of your chopine."

European High Heel

The invention of the high heel is usually attributed to Catherine de Medici, who launched it on Paris in the 1500s. Catherine was the daughter of the distinguished Florentine family and went to Paris in 1533 to marry the future Henry II of France. Being petite, she had several pairs of high-heeled shoes designed by an Italian shoemaker to make her look taller. The style took the French court by storm and soon spread through the European aristocracy.

In the 1600s, the English parliament passed an Act threatening: "Any woman who, through the use of high heeled shoes or other devices, leads a subject of Her Majesty into marriage, shall be punished with the penalties of witchery."

In his autobiography *My Life*, the famous Italian lover Giovanni Casanova recorded his love of high heels. He eulogized about them forcing women to raise their hooped skirts as they walked, so showing off their legs.

In the 1800s, a high-class brothel in New Orleans employed a French girl who wore high heels. The heels were in instant success among clients, and Madam Kathy, who ran the brothel, began importing "French heels" direct from Paris for the other girls to wear. "We learned we could double the fees when the girls sashayed around in those high heels," Madam Kathy wrote in her diary. "It gave a look of class to the ass. The men went crazy just watching them. They drank more, paid more, stayed longer and came back more often." Other bordellos caught on, and American men began urging their wives to wear this enticing new fashion. Eventually, in 1880, a factory making high heels was established in Massachusetts.

Higher Trends

Early high heels were louis heels that narrowed from the sole, then widened again at the base, but as heels became higher, they also became straighter. By the turn of this century, foot specialists were warning against this dangerous trend. Higher, straighter heels were more elegant, but the construction materials available were pushed to their limits, so heels could not get higher—yet. Some female academics condemned high heels in the 1920s and 1930s. But George Bernard Shaw advised women: "If you rebel against high heeled shoes, take care to do so in a very smart hat."

The Second World War posed a more pernicious threat to high heels: leather was rationed. But the resourceful Italian shoe designer Salvatore Ferragamo developed fashion shoes using materials that were cheap and readily available. The corksoled platform shoe was born. The platforms were wedge-shaped to

continued on page 56

A romantic floral print on stiletto-heeled court shoes that are trimmed with the popular "flat bow". They were designed by Roger Vivier in 1960 for Christian Dior.

An early version of the high louis stiletto heel, created in France in 1951.

53

Azagury

Joseph Azagury learned the shoe business from customers. He worked in the Rayne shoe department at Harrods in the mid-to-late 1980s where he saw what people were buying and thought he could design shoes that people wanted.

A tan calf court shoe with understated decorative punched toe cap.

A black suede, narrow-toed, zip-legged, fitted boot with high stiletto heels.

Azagury was born in Morocco in the early 1960s and moved, via Paris, to London. After his stint in the Rayne shoe department in Harrods, he went to the Cordwainers College in London where he studied shoemaking. He worked all over the world before settling back in London, where he went into business with his brother-in-law Robert Zermon. Zermon raised the money to launch the Joseph Azagury line. The design philosophy was to give shoes a handmade feel at affordable prices. It worked and Azagury soon found himself winning 20,000 orders a year.

In 1991, he opened his first store at 73 Knightsbridge, in London, across the street from his brother's boutique. Joseph Azagury makes elegant, understated women's shoes, though his designs are often bold. His square toes and corkscrew heels are striking, but he is known particularly for his simple, sensual sandals with their flowing lines. He has also introduced a line of men's shoes through his London store and has a line of bags made in Italy.

Azagury insists that he does not target a specific type of customer. "I have tried designing with a type of person in mind and it hasn't sold," he says. "At the end of the day, I have to do what I like and trust those feelings." He says that his typical customer is a sophisticated, fashionable girl, who is not too over the top and doesn't want to spend too much. In practice this includes women from 18 to 60, from secretaries to supermodels. His distinguished clientele includes model Marie Helvin, actress Susannah York and singer Nathalie Cole.

Azagury has a factory in Minorca, which employs 18 people. From there it is easy to source high quality materials in Spain and highshine leathers in Italy. As well as making his own shoes and running his own shop, Azagury supplies other stores across the U.K., including Harrods, where he started out. He also exhibits widely to stay in touch with his overseas customers in the U.S. and Europe. Fashion magazines such as *Elle* and *Vogue* are very keen to feature his shoes.

Although his shoes already sell worldwide, Azagury is keen to expand his retail business. He is opening more stores in the U.K. and is set to expand in the U.S., Australasia and the Far East. He is not only a talented designer but also a talented businessman who is ready and eager to take on the world.

Modern version of a 1930s silhouette (*above*), and red suede, ankle-strapped court shoe (*below*).

support the weight of the wearer. Wedge soles went out of fashion quickly after the Second World War. In 1947, the New Look brought femininity back into vogue and Christian Dior's full, ankle-length skirts threw attention back on the foot. The cycle of fashion had moved on, and there was a reaction against practical shoes with thick soles. What the fashion buyer craved once more was elegance.

Elegant Engineering

Shoemakers were already working on the more architectural styles inspired by Dior's highly structured fashions. A sandal with tiny straps and a high, elegant heel was developed by the Italians. The delicate, yet highly engineered look of these shoes complemented Dior's New Look perfectly. They were also powerfully erotic, leaving the foot naked while the rest of the body was conspicuously covered. Shoe designers such as Ferragamo, André Perugia, and Charles Jourdan entered a challenging race to develop the slimmest, most elegant heel.

The problem was that wood, the traditional material of heels, was not strong enough. It could not take the stress that was inflicted by such narrow tapering heels, and the heels frequently snapped. One inventive company tried dipping their heels in a vat of molten copper. The thin sheath of metal around the heel gave greater strength, and other manufacturers followed suit. Ferragamo used brass and even gold to make heels, but these metals were soft, and if the heel was made too thin, it could not support the wearer's weight.

Several designers developed the idea of encasing a steel pin in plastic. Steel was the only material that, when pared down to an elegant spike, could bear a woman's weight. The steel pin of the 1950s freed shoe design, the stiletto reached for the sky, and Vivier took the credit.

Two Italian manufacturers, Del Co and Albanese of Rome, had developed similar styles. Albanese's design was even more radical. The company produced an evening

A 1931 Perugia fish-shaped stiletto, made for Jourdan of France

Plain court shoes with stiletto heels, designed by Ferragamo in 1960. Shoes like this were worn widely in the early 1960s.

Sling-back stilettos by Italian designer Ferragamo of Florence. They have an openwork floral design around the toes, and the piping, sling-backs, and heels have a gold metallic finish.

sandal with two tiny straps and a heel set very far forward, under the arch of the foot. The heel curved backward so that its tip was under the center of the heel. With the help of an aeronautical engineer, Vivier managed to outdo this by curling heels into the shape of commas.

Despite the Italians' contribution, the eyes of the fashion world were focused on Dior, so Vivier got the credit for the stiletto. This is not altogether unfair as Vivier also moved away from the sandal and began to enclose the foot, producing the classic stiletto-heeled pump. He balanced the pointed heel with a pointed toe known as the needle toe. He also encrusted his designs with jewels and embroidery in a lavish style that rivaled anything the 1700s had produced.

While Vivier created the style, the Italian manufacturers made the shoes for the mass market. The U.S. was the home of mechanized shoe manufacture and had traditionally made its own shoes. But by 1957, the U.S. had become a net importer of shoes, with the bulk of fashion shoes coming from Italy. They were plainer than the Parisian handmade originals, but the Italians refined the style down to its essential elements, revealing the underlying elegance of the unadorned stiletto. It was obvious that, while the French could not be rivaled in clothes, the Italians were the shoemakers. They had the craftsmen and the tradition, and were the masters of mass shoe production.

Companies in Europe and America sensed that the Italians were showing the way ahead. The Swiss company Bally, Russell & Bromley in Britain, and Delman and Saks

"Untitled" (*right*), an airbrush picture by Allen Jones in which stiletto heels that raise the foot vertically underpin his erotic vision of women. The original is more than life-size.

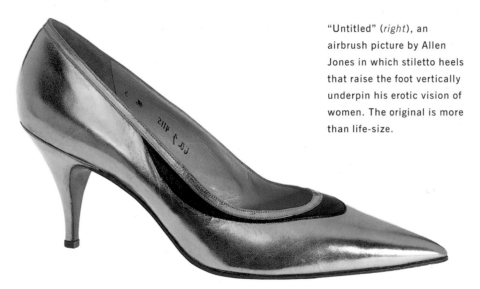

Gold and black evening court shoes produced by Swiss company Bally in 1961, made of kid leather. This style was very popular in the early 1960s.

Stiletto subculture

In the sexually repressed 1950s, a whole subculture sprang up around the stiletto. Specialist manufacturers made shoes with 7 inch (18cm) heels that raised the foot practically vertical. Airbrush artist Allen Jones translated the eroticism of the stiletto into art. Illustrator Antonio Lopez drew women metamorphosing into stiletto-heeled shoes, while American photographer Robert Mapplethorpe depicted models devouring them.

Prada

In the early 1970s, Italian Miuccia Prada, was a feminist politician and a card-carrying Communist. In 1978 she inherited the family firm. In less than a decade, she turned a small Florentine leather goods manufacturer into one of the hottest names in fashion.

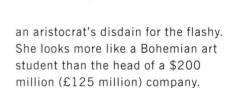

Even when Miuccia Prada was taking to the barricades in her youth, she had an instinctive feel for fashion. "I began to realize that whatever I was wearing, others would start wearing after two or three years."

In 1978, she put politics behind her and joined the family leather goods firm, which had been founded by her grandfather in 1913. Her first revolution in the business was to abandon leather altogether. She designed her now famous nylon rucksack, which was made from parachute fabric. She liked technical fabric and simply decided to make it up into a bag. There was no real reason; she just felt it was right.

Prada's trademark are her square-toed boots. They are part of her little girl look that has set the fashion business on its head. She has fans in the most unlikely quarters. Lesbian-chic pop singer k.d. lang, for example, claims to have discovered Prada by accident. She says that Prada's appeal has to do with confidence and authority instead of vulnerability and typical sexiness. *Vogue* sees it as Prada's innate ability to make women feel womanly without cheapening or objectifying them, a consequence of her deeply held views.

As part of her retro revolution, Prada reintroduced the classic slide and boot, and the sweet, girlish T-

The hottest name in fashion, during the mid-90s produced fast, fun, and often funky ideas to catch the eye.

bar shoe. Critics accuse her of trying to recreate the 1950s, but she feels that things are not changing dramatically at the moment and that this is more a period of reflection. She has said that in the 1950s, life was changing drastically, everybody was thinking new things, looking to the future. In the 1960s and 1970s, there were revolutionary changes going on. But now, there's nothing very exciting. "We can't create revolutionary dresses in a world that isn't revolutionary, fashion is a reflection of the life we are living," she says. However, she believes that the rediscovery of a new femininity is a serious trend and that her company set it in motion.

In footwear, she tries to create a new balance between styles and lines that echo the past, but become modern when rendered in new fabrics and colors. She sees this as the research for a new kind of sportswear. About 30 percent of the Prada business is now in clothes, 50 percent in bags and accessories, and only 20 percent in footwear. But although the pieces are shown together, there is little crossover. "Each piece has to stand alone," she says. "This is what we call 'product'." Miuccia Prada herself has

an aristocrat's disdain for the flashy. She looks more like a Bohemian art student than the head of a $200 million (£125 million) company.

It is said that you won't seen her designs at the Oscars, or at movie premieres. But when Princess Caroline of Monaco is snapped by a paparazzi for *Hello!* magazine, actress Natasha Richardson goes shopping in the rain, they will be wearing Prada.

Prada's inspirational love of fashion seems set to continue. For her, going to buy something or try something on, is one of the pleasures of life.

This much-copied designer label produced a new narrow toe with narrow-based heel for its 1997-98 collections.

Low stilettos (*left*) from Raphael of Rome, 1962.

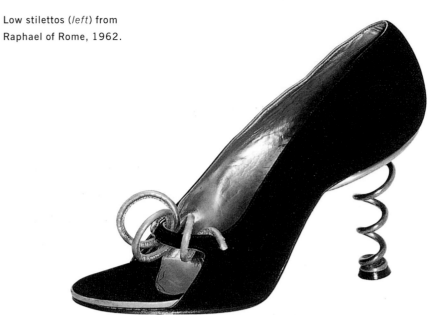

Fifth Avenue of New York began selling lightweight sandals with narrow straps and high heels that became the standard fare for fashionable women.

A 1962 Perugia stiletto for Jourdan of France, this time with a corkscrew heel.

Stilettos and Sex Goddesses

Pointed stiletto-heeled pumps and slingbacks were the footwear of choice of the screen sex goddesses. Italian shoes were extremely popular among movie stars, partly because of Ferragamo's connections with Hollywood. Brigitte Bardot and Elizabeth Taylor were soon sporting needle-sharp stilettos, and Jayne Mansfield had more than 200 pairs. In the 1956 movie *High Society*, Frank Sinatra sipped champagne from a stiletto pump, and in 1960 Anita Ekberg paddled in the Trevi Fountain, stilettos in hand, in *La Dolce Vita*.

Ferragamo produced stilettos for Sophia Loren, though he rounded the toe for comfort. Perugia refined the design still further, until his sandals consisted of a wafer-thin sole with tiny straps and a perilously thin question-mark-shaped heel made of a steel alloy plated with gold. Marilyn Monroe said simply: "I don't know who invented the high heel, but all women owe him a lot... It was the high heel that gave the big lift to my career."

The stiletto heel certainly helped give Marilyn that wiggle to her walk, but she had a secret. To increase the hipswinging action her heels gave her, she had one heel made slightly shorter than the other. With Mansfield, Monroe, and the other sex bombs of the

"Madeleine", a 1961 stiletto-heeled court shoe produced by Bally. This one is in brown suede with black patent leather toecap, heel, and three tiny boot buttons.

Well heeled

One effect of stilettos was the damage they did to floors. In stilettos, a woman's weight was concentrated on two tiny points, which literally drilled into the ground. They left holes and dents wherever the woman walked. Newly fashionable polished woodblock flooring was particularly vulnerable. Valuable carpets were also ruined, and the tarmac in the city streets of Mediterranean countries was inevitably studded with pockmarks. Stilettos were soon banned from public buildings, and even from airplanes, supposedly for safety reasons. Another common hazard for fashionable women was getting a stiletto caught in street grating.

A pair of scarlet satin, stiletto-heeled evening shoes, created by London designer Jimmy Choo in 1997. To enhance their effect they have long ribbons that are designed to be wound alluringly up the legs.

1950s, wearing it, the stiletto heel became firmly linked with sex appeal in the public mind. As the *Saturday Evening Post* newspaper put it:

"The girl with low and sensible heels,
    Is likely to pay for her bed and meals."

Delicately cantilevered stilettos suited the pencil skirts and the pushup bras of the late 1950s as well as they had the fuller fashions of the New Look. Perching precariously on their stilettos, women had learned to walk carefully. Stilettos seemed to give women more poise as they balanced on their slender heels.

Health Hazards

However, the fashion for stilettos in the 1950s was accompanied by dire warnings from the medical profession. All kinds of problems, from gynecological symptoms to juvenile delinquency, were blamed on the stiletto shoe. Doctors brandished foot X-rays, which purported to show the dire effects of wearing such precariously heeled shoes. One foot specialist claimed that a woman would use over twice as much energy to walk in 3-inch. (8cm) heels than in flat shoes. There was talk of bunions, hammer toes, thickening ankles, and prematurely curved spines.

Despite the introduction of new shoe fashions, the stiletto has an enduring appeal. In the 1960s, Batman's arch enemy *Catwoman*, Jane Fonda's *Barbarella*, and Emma Peel in the cult TV series *The Avengers* wore boots with stiletto heels. Stilettos were briefly eclipsed by the return of platforms in the early 1970s. But by the end of the decade, models Beverley Johnson and Jerry Hall were adding to their

Elegant evening sandals with silver and black suede uppers and a thin high heel, created by Yves St Laurent in 1990.

Two styles of stiletto shoe by Italian designer Rossimoda. Created in 1990-91, the black and gold shoe (*left*) has a metal "needle" stiletto. The haute couture shoes (*below*) for Yves St Laurent have a larger metal stiletto and were designed in 1988.

"Cage", a shoe from a winter 1990-91 collection by Andrea Pfister. The "cage" itself is created from suede straps trimmed with gold kidskin.

considerable height, and showing off their long, sinuous legs in strappy sandals with high heels.

The 1980s saw the advent of the power dresser, and stilettos joined the shoulder pad as a symbol of female assertiveness. The fashion was an echo of the origin of the high heel as a symbol of status and power. The top shoe designer Manolo Blahnik made stilettos expensive, which took them away from their tackier associations with sex and prostitution, and gave them a new wit, extravagance, and glamour.

Since then, stilettos have come click-clacking back once again. The stiletto is now seen as the "Wonderbra of the feet," a postfeminist statement that is an overt display of sexuality and femininity. In her book, Boobs, Boys and High Heels, model, actress, and fashion designer Dianne Brill wrote: "High heels are your pedestals. They transform any set of feet into sex symbols, wear them and you show the provocatively purring feline side of your sexuality." If that is the case, then stilettos will be around for a long time to come.

And, to end on a high note, two shoes (*top and above*) from the Charles Jourdan catalog.

Metal-heeled black patent leather court shoes by Chinese Canadian designer Anne Michelle. She created these in 1987.

A pretty and unusual d'orsay cut court shoe with a frill trim, designed in 1990 by Rossimoda for Italian maker Beltrami.

61

5

Sandals

The sandal is one of the oldest and simplest of shoes. It was developed in warm climates and never goes out of fashion because it is so functional. The secret of the evening sandal's glamour is to leave the foot almost naked. The sandal is essentially just a sole attached to the foot by a strap or thong. Experts think that sandals made their first appearance in the Mediterranean around 3000 B.C. An ancient Egyptian victory palette of that period shows the Pharaoh Menes with a servant carrying his

sandals. The oldest surviving example of a sandal also comes from Egypt and was made of woven papyrus in about 2000 B.C. Sandals were also made from leather and wood, and worn only by Egyptians of rank.

Three Egyptian sandals (*above*) in designs that have been around for many hundreds of years. They are made entirely of woven papyrus reed, and each one has a foot strap and a slim toe-post. A Birkenstock sandal (*far right*) with a thick sole and black leather straps.

A FLIMSY FASHION

The ancient Greeks went barefoot indoors, but outdoors they wore sandals with leather, felt, or matting soles, tied on with thongs. Romans wore sandals indoors and out, and some Roman prostitutes had special sandals with soles carved with letters that left the message "Follow me" printed on soft ground. Roman soldiers wore sandals with hobnailed soles. Each legion had its own pattern of nails in the sole, and the best legions were said to use gold nails. Roman sandals were called *"calige"* and the emperor Gaius Caesar was so fond of his that he was known as Caligula. Roman empresses had sandals with soles of gold and straps encrusted with precious stones. These were the forerunners of today's evening sandal.

With the fall of the Roman Empire, sandals largely fell out of favor in the Western world, and were replaced by the closed shoe. They briefly returned to fashion during the Directoire period in France (1795-1799) when everything classical was in vogue. Sandals of the period were blue, white, gold, or silver and held on by ribbons or leather straps. They complemented the flimsy, classically inspired dresses of the time. The fashion for sandals with double soles, called comforts, spread from the Continent to Britain in the early 1800s. Later in the century, the Pre-Raphaelite artists attempted to revive sandals, but by the beginning of the 1900s, they were definitely out of fashion.

Riviera Style

During the 1920s, the writer F. Scott Fitzgerald and his circle made vacationing in the South of France fashionable. In came the suntan, the swimsuit, and the sandal. The couturier Coco Chanel was one of the first to pick up on these trends to go with her new, freer attitude toward clothes, and she created the slingback sandal.

A gray leather evening sandal (*below*) created for Josephine Baker, the American nightclub entertainer. It was inspired by her famous turban and was designed by André Perugia in 1928.

A low-heeled sandal (*right*) made by Bally in 1934. It has cross-over foot straps and ankle straps of red, black and white striped grosgrain ribbon, secured with a decorative gilt buckle fastening.

A pair of Austrian-made sandals from 1934. They have hinged wooden soles and woven canvas straps in bright colors. The ankle strap can be adjusted and there is a bead-trimmed lace fastening across the instep.

André Perugia, who came from the Riviera himself, began to produce elegant high-heeled sandals for evening wear. This was risqué because at the time it was considered indecent for a woman to show off her toes in public during the day. Perugia believed that the way to understand a woman's personality was to study her feet, and to do that they had to be unveiled.

Perugia was at his most daring with his selection of sandals. A master of materials, he made sandals in shiny snakeskin, purple suede, and pearlized lizard. In 1928, he made a sandal for the entertainer Josephine Baker. Its stylized purple leather ankle and toe fastenings resembled the exotic turbans the star wore on her head. Invention did not stop there: in 1929 he made a sandal that looked like a mask, and his 1930 Cubist sandal was so elegantly cantilevered and modernist that it could have been designed by the architect Le Corbusier.

The American Sandal

While Perugia was working in France, Salvatore Ferragamo brought the sandal from Italy to the U.S. His sandal techniques were honed by his work on Cecil B. De Mille's movie, *The Ten Commandments*. In 1923, De Mille commissioned Ferragamo to make over 12,000 pairs of sandals for the movie in less than two months. After a trip to a local library, Ferragamo discovered that very little was known about ancient Egyptian footwear, so he based his designs on some Victorian illustrations.

During the same period, Ferragamo invented his version of the Roman sandal. It fastened around the ankle with a single thong. The revolutionary steel reinforcement he used in his shoes allowed him to create dainty pedestals to show off the foot. In the warm climate of California, his creations quickly caught on as evening wear. And when movie stars wore them on screen, the fashion for elegant evening sandals took off around the world.

The Great Depression of the early 1930s furthered the cause of the sandal. With restricted funds, people took their entertainment outdoors. They went to the beach, took up cycling, and in Europe, naturism became popular. Sandals seemed to epitomize the health-conscious attitude of the time. They were worn on the beach, at parties and, gradually, for chic wear with day clothes. Men wore them too: a 1937 photograph of the British Men's Dress Reform Party, an organization that aimed to free men from the constraints of formal dressing, shows a man wearing T-strap sandals.

Espadrilles

Espadrilles are corded or ropesoled shoes with canvas uppers. They originated in Mediterranean countries, where they were mostly worn by fishermen. They became fashionable leisurewear, along with sandals, in the 1920s and 1930s. John F. Kennedy was photographed wearing espadrilles while on vacation in 1938, and Salvador Dali and Picasso were constant wearers. With the fashion for Mediterranean vacations in the 1960s, espadrilles were essential summer wear. And in 1973, they became fashionable party wear for young women, held on by long ribbons that laced up the leg.

A pair of gold leather evening sandals with low platform soles and sturdy heels. The ankle strap is fastened with an unassuming buckle. They were made in the 1940s.

Coco Chanel

Gabrielle "Coco" Chanel opened her first shop, in Deauville, France, in 1913 and by the end of the First World War had developed the simple "poor girl" look using jersey fabric. Chanel had caught the mood of the time, something she would do repeatedly throughout her career. She moved to Paris where she dominated the world of haute couture for 60 years. At the height of her career, she would employ 3,500 people.

Chanel introduced black sandals with velvet toes, black satin pumps with crystal buckles, and sophisticated patent evening shoes. In 1935, French *Vogue* showed her evening gowns with flatheeled black satin shoes, an idea later adopted by many designers in the 1980s.

In 1957, Chanel's shoemaker Raymond Massaro designed a new twotone slingback shoe. The beige court shoe with black toecap and heel made the foot seem smaller. With its straight, set back heel and slim toe this design offered a comfortable yet stylish alternative to the stiletto, and was widely copied.

Although Chanel retired in 1938, she returned in 1954 to create the classic Chanel suit with its cardigan jacket trimmed with braid and matching skirt. "I make fashions that women can live in, breathe in, feel comfortable in and look younger in," she said. Coco Chanel died in 1971, at the age of 87, in her apartment in the Ritz in Paris.

Pimento red leather sandals with pleated detail and matching bag. Designed by Americans Rayne and Jay Herbert in 1977, the heels have a winged angel in relief.

On the Street

The fashion for sandals had an effect on the more formal court shoe. In 1936, the opentoed shoe was introduced and was an immediate success. The slingback quickly followed, but they could not compete with the sandal, which was seen everywhere, even on city streets. *Vogue* was outraged and declared that wearing sandals in the street displayed a lack of good taste and was unhygenic and bad for the feet. In July 1939, *Vogue* sent a cameraman out on Fifth Avenue, Manhattan, to photograph the feet of women in the street. The magazine published the pictures throughout the world to show "how women look on the sidewalks of New York in toeless, backless, highheeled slippers…*Vogue* still maintains that women who really have taste and a knowledge of the fitness of things do not wear them for walking the city streets."

But it was the Second World War, not *Vogue*'s fit of pique that halted the relentless march of the sandal. They suddenly seemed to leave the foot too exposed and vulnerable in a hostile world. In a short time leather shortages and wartime restrictions produced stouter and more practical footwear.

The Inventive Maestro

In Italy, wartime shortages only made Ferragamo more inventive. When leather was commandeered to make soldiers' boots, he used raffia, crocheted cellophane, woven grass, and packing string to make witty and unusual sandals. The lack of materials forced the designer to be sparing so his sandal straps became progressively thinner and more elegant. He began to use cork for the soles and so created the wedge.

After the war, Italy became the centre of shoe fashion. Many Italian manufacturers began to produce delicately strapped sandals with high heels. Their response to the longer skirts of Christian Dior's "New Look" was to expose as much of the foot as possible.

Always ahead of the trend, Ferragamo made an "invisible" sandal in 1947. The vamp was made out of a single transparent nylon thread that passed

A wedge-heeled, sling-back sandal (*right*) with a Turkish slipper look, created by French designer Heyrault in the 1940s.

Robert Clergerie

"What counts is not fashion, but style, because fashion goes out of fashion but style never does." That is the design philosophy of one of France's top contemporary shoe designer, Robert Clergerie, who is known for his futuristic footwear. Robert Clergerie came to shoe design late in life. He had a career as an army officer before graduating from the Ecole Supérieure de Commerce in Paris. This led him to a management post in the renowned French shoe company Charles Jourdan, where he headed the Xavier Danaud footwear division.

In 1978, Clergerie bought a small shoe company and set about restructuring it. He soon realized that to get his ideas across he would have to design the company's shoes himself and in 1981 he launched a line under his own name. His shoes have clean, architectural lines and always seem to be forward looking, though he is not averse to reinterpreting earlier styles. Clergerie's futuristic attitudes and his experimentation with laminated metal soles have made him a role model for younger shoe designers. When he was in his fifties, Clergerie was making the bold innovations most designers make in their twenties. His innovative spirit was recognized in the U.S. in 1992 when he was honored with the Fashion Footwear Association of New York Design Award. His approach is simple: the stronger the idea, the less need there is for decoration. The result is that he makes classics. There are now three labels in the Clergerie stable. Robert Clergerie Signature shoes are elegant and expensive, Espace is a younger, more casual line, while Joseph Festrier is a line of shoes for men, featuring the traditional Goodyear welt construction. As well as designing shoes, Clergerie manages and administers his own company which now turns over more than $30 million (£19 million) a year.

Below, a selection of Clergerie's designs: *far left,* a simple black leather sandal decorated with gray fabric and silver studs, *centre,* a slingback in pale pastel colored snakeskin. *Right,* foot-wrapping sandal in rainbow-colored snakeskin.

repeatedly over the instep. More loops of clear nylon formed a slingback, leaving the foot almost completely nude. The wedged sole, covered with either red or gold kid, and the heel were pared away so that, from some angles, the feet appeared to be floating. Ferragamo said the idea came as he watched men fishing on the River Arno in Florence and realised their transparent fishing line could be used to make a vamp.

Despite this virtuoso performance, the "invisible" sandal did not sell well. Ferragamo later came to believe that it left women feeling too exposed. The sandal reappeared in many guises in the following decades, but never really took off. Charles Jourdan's version in the 1980s had a flat sole and clear acrylic upper, decorated with plastic fruit, but it suffered the same fate of its predecessors. The public, it seems, likes the legend of Cinderella's glass slipper but does not want to wear it.

The Sandal Triumphant

The 1950 fashion for Italian sandals was so popular that court shoes appeared with all sorts of cut outs and straps. Top designers, such as Valentino, created flat sandals for summer wear, and slides, with either a woven net or a network of leather straps, appeared. Ferragamo's version was the Kimo sandal. Made in gold kid, a basket of crisscrossed straps rose high up the instep. It was an instant success.

A pair of sandals with open-structured brass heels and black satin uppers created by Ferragamo took pride of place on the Italian stand at an exhibition in London in 1955 to promote a united Europe. Then in 1957, Ferragamo created a pair of sandals with delicate 18-carat gold chain uppers and soles and heels covered in a thin layer

continued page 70

A sculptural sandal created by André Perugia in 1950. It was inspired by Pablo Picasso's Cubist work, and is made of leather, wood and metal.

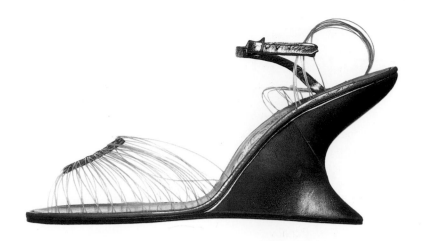

Salvatore Ferragamo

A 1947 design. The sole and ankle strap are in gold kid leather, with a superstructure in transparent nylon thread to give the illusion of a bare foot. This sandal is one of the last Ferragamo designed with a wedge heel.

As a small boy Salvatore Ferragamo knew that he had a vocation to make shoes. Twenty-five years after his death, he was honored with an exhibition celebrating his life and work in Florence. The show went on to tour the world but millions had already seen his shoe creations in the movies. He was responsible for Greta Garbo's flatheeled brogues and Marilyn Monroe's stilettos.

A 1939 design with black velvet uppers, a multilayered platform and a through sole. It is much lighter than it looks.

Salvatore Ferragamo was born in 1898 in Bonito, in southern Italy, the eleventh of 14 children. His father was a small landowner and Ferragamo had to leave school at the age of nine. Despite the family's poverty, his father looked down on his ambition to make shoes. Cobbling was consider a lowly trade confined to the humblest section of society but Ferragamo was determined and apprenticed himself to the village cobbler in Bonito. The first shoes he made was a white pair for his little sister's first communion.

By the age of 14, Ferragamo had his own workshop and employed six people. The women of Bonito, who had previously gone to Naples for their shoes, flocked to his shop. He could have stayed in Bonito happily making shoes for the rest of his life, but his older brother Alfonsino had emigrated to America and wrote home describing the machines of the Queen Quality Shoe Company in Boston, which produced thousands of pairs of shoes a day. Ferragamo had to see for himself, but when he arrived in America Ferragamo did not like what he saw. machinemade American shoes seemed to him heavy, clumsy, and graceless.

Ferragamo set up a shop in Santa Barbara where he made shoes by hand, to order, the Italian way. The propman from the American Film Company ordered some boots from him for a Western. The director Cecil B. De Mille was impressed and Ferragamo began getting huge orders to make the shoes for historical epics and costume dramas. There is no record of how much Ferragamo charged for these shoemaking epics, but they gave him enough money to buy the Hollywood Boot Shop on the then-fashionable Hollywood

Boulevard, opposite Grauman's Chinese Theatre. The movie stars also began buying their shoes from him. Mary Pickford, Douglas Fairbanks, Rudolf Valentino, John Barrymore, Clara Bow, Pola Negri, Gloria Swanson, and Barbara La Marr were all customers and, in 1923, Ferragamo moved to Hollywood to be nearer his clientele.

But Ferragamo was not content. He took a course in chemistry at the University of Pennsylvania to develop new techniques of dyeing leather and attended medical lectures at Los Angeles University to improve his understanding of the foot. He developed a new system for measuring the foot so he could make his shoes more comfortable. He reinforced the soles of his shoes with a thin sheet of steel that allowed them to be delicate yet strong.

Ferragamo soon found that there were not the craftsmen in America to maintain the quality of his handmade work. In 1927, he returned to Italy and settled in Florence. His workshop there was soon supplying the top shoe stores in the U.S. and Britain. After the Wall Street Crash, Ferragamo had to close down his

A 1938 design in multi-colored woven raffia with taselled ties. Prior to this, raffia had only been used by the poor, but Ferragamo made it acceptable in haute couture.

business, but he continued making shoes, drawing inspiration from recent archeological discoveries in Egypt, and the art movement, Futurism. He paid off his debts and set up in business again, this time employing apprentices whom he trained for the future.

In 1935, following Italy's invasion of Abyssinia, the League of Nations imposed strict economic sanctions on Italy. Ferragamo soon found it impossible to import the high quality materials he needed to make luxury shoes and he began to improvise with raffia, string, and cellophane. He could no longer get the steel he needed to reinforce his shoes, so he developed the cork wedge, which took America by storm.

In 1947, Ferragamo was honored by Neiman Marcus, alongside Christian Dior, Irene of Hollywood, and the Queen of England's couturier Norman Hartnell. That same year, he abandoned the wedge and went to work on a thinner high heel better suited to Christian Dior's "New Look." Sophia Loren, Audrey Hepburn, the Duchess of Windsor, and Princess Maria Pia of Savoy were all customers. Again demand outstripped supply and Ferragamo had to turn 40 percent of his production over to machinemade shoes. In 1960, Ferragamo wrote his autobiography. Its title would make a fitting epitaph — he called it *Shoemaker of Dreams.* He died later that year.

This sandal is decorated in 18-carat gold, and cost $1,000 when it was created in 1956. The straps are twisted gold chains and the heel has scroll decoration.

Beth and Herbert Levine

Like David Evins, Beth Levine worked at I. Miller in the U.S. in the 1940s. In 1950, she married Herbert Levine, a salesman and shoe designer, and left to form the company Beth and Herbert Levine. The company came to the fore in the 1960s, when Herbert produced clear plastic shoes and gold mules with long gold toes that coiled around ending in a jeweled flourish. Beth's contribution was to introduce bamboo to shoemaking.

The couple were open to the influence of pop art and produced shoes that looked like sports cars or Aladdin's lamps. In 1967, they won the Coty Award for their stretch boot. Later, they attached clear acrylic heels and soles to pantyhose, creating all-in-one boots and pants. They designed slippers with rolled and stacked heels, and won the Neiman Marcus Award for their contribution to the industry. Although their company no longer exists, they remain a huge influence on shoe design.

The fully open toe and the ankle strap on a closed back were popular in the late 1970s and early 1980s.

of gold. Back in Hollywood, David Evins took over the business of producing sandals for the stars. In 1934, he made a pair for Claudette Colbert in Cecil B. De Mille's *Cleopatra*. They had a sculpted wedge sole, covered in multicolor pavé. The single strap was a long gold tube attached to the sole near the toes and hooked around the heel, the two sides joining over the instep. Ten years later, he modified the designed for streetwear. Then, in 1963, he was commissioned to make a new line of sandals for Elizabeth Taylor's *Cleopatra*. When he wasn't working on a film, he made sandals for stars such as Ava Gardner and Lena Horne.

In the 1950s, Roger Vivier made a Parisian version of the décolleté sandal, with a high heel. His were more ornate than those of other designers, and he left himself large side panels to decorate with silver pavé. The ankle and toe straps were also thicker, giving the shoe an air of respectability. In contrast, the American Beth Levine began producing flat-heeled sandals in clear acrylic.

In the 1960s, the sandal went low-heel and lightweight, and Italian shoe manufacturer Bruno Magli began decorating them. Jewelry, butterflies, bows, and fruit appeared on the strap across the instep. Ethnic sandals, especially those from India, became part of the hippie look. In Italy, Mario Valentino responded with a line of classical sandals that rose up the calf, like those of Roman legionaries. Chain stores emulated them with versions that laced up the leg.

The elegant, high-heeled evening sandal struggled on. Perugia was still making them in the 1960s. In the prow toe version, created in 1960, the sole was sculptured so that the ball of the foot sank into it and the heel and toe were raised above it. Beth Levine also created a sandal with a sculptured sole, fastened with a simple ankle and toe strap.

Whimsy and Color

Evening sandals were raised on huge platforms in the 1970s. The 1980s brought them down to earth again with flatter, leather sandals and new colorful versions of the high, strappy styles that gave minimum coverage. In 1979, Swiss shoe designer Andrea Pfister produced the "Deauville," a low-heeled, open basketweave sandal made in plastic. It is said to have been copied more than any other shoe. He also produced a high-heeled sandal with bright blocks of color on the sole, heel and

An Andrea Pfister design from 1989, entitled "Mille et une nuits". The toe-post is enriched with multicolored stones set in gilt.

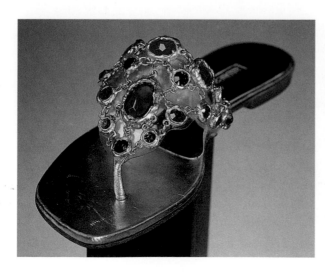

Herbert Levine's 1965 leaf sandals. They have adhesive pads that stick to the feet, and no uppers. They never caught on.

fastenings, which he called "Homage to Mondrian." In a fit of whimsy, he created a flat 1920s-style beach sandal with a foot painted on the inner sole and a small beach umbrella decorating the strap.

Sandals for the 1990s

Salvatore Ferragamo's daughter Fiamma had stepped into her father's shoes, and by the 1990s was producing elegant highheeled sandals every bit as inventive as her father's. In England, Patrick Cox produced his evening sandals in gold with large, knotted slingbacks. He had tried to persuade men to wear the enclosed sandal with a T-strap and buckle, but had to contend with the sandal's schoolboy image.

Cox likes to take chances though, and he began experimenting with molded plastic jelly. Children had worn plastic sandals for decades, but taking inspiration from French fishermen's sandals, Cox turned them into brash street wear for young adults. This type of molded plastic sandal ran like a tidal wave through the chain stores in 1995.

In the mid-1990s, the vamp sandal came into fashion. This was essentially a hybrid of the court shoe and the sandal. It had far too much upper to be a true sandal, but too little to be considered an enclosed shoe. Meanwhile, designer Bernard Figueroa demonstrated that the sandal could still be sexy. In 1994, he showed a high-heel sandal with straps that tied around the ankles. The uppers were smothered in fabric flowers.

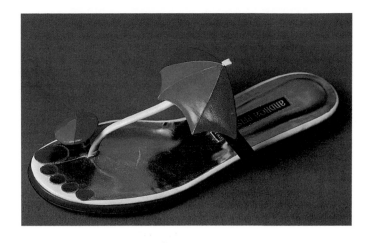

Andrea Pfister designed this sandal in 1984 and christened it "Capri", as it was inspired by the Italian island of that name in the Bay of Naples. The open parasol and five-toed imprint conjour up the feel of a hot Mediterranean beach.

A 1972 design by Herbert Levine (above). The straps are enlivened by diamanté-centred, colored fabric discs.

Created by Red or Dead in 1997, these lightweight shoes (*left*) have waterproof fabric uppers with velcro.

A modern sports sandal (below) made using modern synthetic materials.

A double-strap buckled sandle in gray leather.

6

Clogs, Platforms, & Wedges

Wooden shoes were often seen as workwear, suitable only for the poor, but in this century, clogs, platform shoes and wedges left this image behind to scale new heights of fashion. The clog is a shoe made from hardwood. Traditionally, it was a working shoe and there are two basic types. The Dutch clog is simply a block of wood that has been hollowed out and shaped to follow the contours of the foot. The design has remained much the same for 600 years. The English clog is a variation on the Dutch clog with a shaped wooden sole that has an upper tacked on to it. The upper is usually leather, but raffia, canvas and other types of fabric can also be used. From these basic wooden shoe types have evolved the huge variety of "bulky" shoe types we know today.

A forerunner of today's platform shoe (*above*), this is a red velvet platform mule, worn by a lady of nobility in Venice, Italy, in around 1590. Shoes were originally designed with such high soles to prevent long dresses from trailing in the wet and mud, but they soon became a fashionable item in their own right, and rapidly became higher and higher. They reached the absurd height of 9 inch (22 cm) before being banned, following innumerable accidents. The modern clog (*opposite*), with a suede upper and wood and rubber sole, is one offshoot from this Venetian design, and is undoubtedly a lot more practical.

A SOLE OF DISCRETION

The soles of platform shoes are usually made from cork or manmade styrene. The soles of platform shoes are from ½—8 inches (1.3—20 cm) thick and raises the ball of the foot, as well as the heel. The heel and the sole tend to be two separate units. Like stilettos, the platform shoe can trace its origins back to the raised wood chopines of 16th-century Venice. The wedge shoe also uses a cork sole to raise the foot, but the sole and heel are all in one piece. The definition is not very strict, though. Wedges sometimes have part of the sole cut out under the arch of the foot, but still tend to have a thicker arch than the platform shoe.

The English, or Lancashire, clog or patten made an appearance among the wealthy in the 1600s. Samuel Pepys complains in his diary on 24 January 1660: "Called on my wife and took her to Mrs Pierce's, she in the way being exceedingly troubled with a pair of new pattens and I vexed to go so slow, it being late." Pattens were wooden overshoes designed to protect good shoes from the mired streets, but they were a fashion item too. The Baroque painter Caspar Netscher depicted a pair of woodensoled shoes with smart black leather uppers, fashionable square toes and cutaway sides in his 1664 painting *The Lace Maker*. In 1694, Queen Mary II of England bought five pairs of satin sabots, or clogs, with gold and silver lacing. Men also wore clogs and, around that time, a pair of men's short clog boots was advertised in the *London Gazette*.

A poulaine with a carved wooden sole and elongated toe. These were worn as overshoes to protect the fabric footwear that was commonly worn before leather shoes were introduced. This example comes from Amsterdam, Holland, and was made around 1375.

A French design from the late 1930s by Preciosa—Herault. This evening shoe has a wedge heel and is in midnight-blue satin with a cord stitch, trimmed with silver leather. Throughout the 1920s and 1930s, fabric and leather shoes were the most popular choice for relaxed evening wear.

Created in 1945 and christened "Pepenie" by the New Jersey company that made them, these high-heeled gold leather sandals have extreme platform soles. The design was an exciting departure after the austerity of the war years, but what is even more intriguing is that they could still be part of the 1990s fashion scene.

Dancing Shoes

In 20th-century England, clogs first came into fashion as dancing shoes. Clog dancing had developed on the cobbled streets of northern cities during the 1800s and remained a popular entertainment there until the Second World War. The dancer, invariably a man, created complex rhythms by tapping the toes and heels of his clogs on the cobblestones.

Clogdancing troupes toured music halls in northern England at the end of the 1800s. Charlie Chaplin got one of his first breaks when he joined J.W. Jackson's troupe called Eight Lancashire Lads, in 1896. These troupes began touring America, where clog dancing quickly transformed into tap dancing. The original tap shoes were a type of clog and the metal jingles were added to the sole later. In America, lines of chorus girls tap danced wearing special shoes know as Mary-Janes. These were kept in place with an ankle strap fastened with a button or buckle. This style spread out into fashion shoes generally.

These shoes, made in England during the Second World War, have stacked wedge heels and are in brown suede with snakeskin tongues.

Herman B. Delman

The leading U.S. shoemaker Herman B. Delman was born in Portersville, California, in 1895, and educated in Portland, Oregon, where his parents owned a small shoe store. After serving in the Marines in the First World War, he opened a shoe store in Hollywood, another on Madison Avenue, New York and one within Saks. From the late 1930s, he worked closely with the store Bergdorf Goodman.

Delman encouraged young designers, and hired them to make shoes for his shop windows. In 1938, he began making shoes for Roger Vivier, while Vivier was still in Paris. When Vivier fled to New York during the Second World War Delman employed him and represented him worldwide for many years.

Delman sold out to the retail giant Genesco in the 1950s, and Edward Rayne, his partner in an English store since the 1930s, took over the business. In 1961, Genesco sold half the business to Rayne, on the proviso that he ran it for the next 10 years. Rayne built the annual sales to over a billion-and-a-half pairs. In 1973, the English retail chain Debenhams bought Rayne-Delman.

Vivienne Westwood

John Fairchild, of Women's Wear Daily, believes that Vivienne Westwood is one of few living fashion geniuses. She was the first British designer since Mary Quant to be invited to show her collection in Paris. But at home in Britain, Westwood is often dismissed as eccentric.

To some Westwood is the Queen of British Fashion. To others she is a designer with a mission to shock who makes clothes that no one will wear and shoes not even veteran catwalk model Naomi Campbell can walk in. Born in 1941, Westwood was a teacher when she met pop entrepreneur Malcolm McLaren in 1971. Together they set up a boutique in London's World's End called *Let It Rock*, which sold 1950s-style clothes

The following year, they changed the name of the shop to *Too Fast to Live, Too Young to Die*, a slogan taken from the bikers' jacket. They sold not just leather bikers' gear, but also the leather outfits associated with sadomasochistic sex. In 1974, they changed the name of the store again, this time to *Sex*, and Westwood brought out a bondage collection. Working mainly in black leather and rubber, she covered her clothes with straps, zippers, studs, chains and buckles. Her shoes also featured multiple zippers, straps and buckles. She produced tortuously high stilettos and leopard print pumps, always exploring the erotic potential of the outer limits of fashion.

Westwood's bondage trousers and ripped T-shirts became the street style of the punk era, launched by McLaren and the band Sex Pistols.

McLaren went on to pursue a career in the music industry in America, leaving Westwood in London with the shop. She changed its name again, to Seditionaires. Her aim, she said, was political. She wanted to "seduce people into revolt".

In 1981, Westwood left punk behind and pioneered the New Romantics movement. She produced her "Pirates" collection which established her a major designer. Historic revivalism has remained a major theme of her work. In 1985, she revived the crinoline as the "mini-crin". Sex is another constant. In 1994, she pared her model's outfit down to a G-string and a bunch of flowers. And she is not ashamed to be seen in her own risqué creations. She appeared at a reception at Kensington Palace wearing a see-through dress with nothing on underneath.

Westwood has a capacity for seizing ideas from different eras of history and throwing them together to make a post-modernist collage. In Westwood's world, kilts can be bright pink, stockings rubber, bras can be worn outside dresses and models can be dressed in mud-splattered, torn clothing with rags in their hair.

In footwear, Vivienne Westwood is most famous for the 7 inch (18 cm) platforms that the model Naomi Campbell toppled from in Paris. She followed that with the Prostitute Shoe, a gold pump with a dainty character strap, a love-heart buckle, and a 7 inch (18 cm) stiletto.

The silhouette which sent supermodel Naomi Campbell tumbling to the floor. A pair now resides in London's Victoria & Albert Museum. This version in lime green is designed to complement the "slip of a dress."

The Craze for Wedges and Platforms

The French shoe designer Roger Vivier is said to have invented the platform in the mid 1930s. He got the idea from orthopedic shoes, originally designed for medical purposes. When Vivier sent his creation to his manufacturer, the U.S. shoemaker Herman B. Delman, Delman sent a telegram in reply, saying: "Are you crazy?" Delman may not have appreciated what Vivier was doing, but the designer Schiaparelli did and she helped launch the fashion for platforms which swept through America in the 1940s.

It was the Italians who launched the wedge. In July 1938, *Harper's Bazaar* reported: "Whereas French women only wear orthopedic sandals in the house or on the beach, Italian women have literally gone mad about the wedge."

The man responsible was the Italian shoe designer Salvatore Ferragamo. In 1936, he patented his first wedge—an evening sandal with a vamp consisting of two straps of black satin and gold calf. The ankle strap was made of the same material and securely fastened with a buckle. A mosaic of gilded glass covered the wedge, which had a leather sole.

For 10 years, Ferragamo had been making dainty, elegant shoes with steel reinforcement in the sole. But when war broke out with Abyssinia, steel was unobtainable in Italy and Ferragamo began to use cork instead. To produce the

A clever idea (*below*) in which the laminations often seen in platform soles are picked up in the design of the heel and the closed heel back. The shoe was created by Ferragamo in 1938.

A shoe designed in 1942 by Luigi Bufarini of Rome (*below*), Italy. This high-fashion shoe in stitched silver leather seems an unlikely product of the war years, and the chopine-like silhouette would not be out of place today.

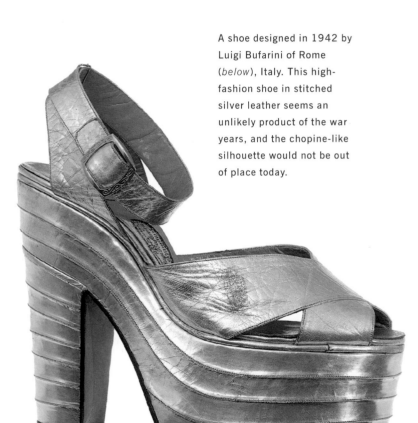

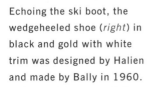

Echoing the ski boot, the wedgeheeled shoe (*right*) in black and gold with white trim was designed by Halien and made by Bally in 1960.

Worn by film star Gloria Swanson, these black satin and gold leather shoes were created by Herbert Levine in the early 1960s. The platform and elongated heel give a Japanese feel.

strength he required, he pressed and glued layers of cork together, creating the wedge. The style was reviled at first, then copied, eventually becoming Ferragamo's most popular model. Its sole was particularly comfortable, giving the wearer the sensation she was walking on cushions. Ferragamo also began making a number of platform sandals for day wear. The platforms were made of wood and decorated in bright colors and abstract patterns. There was only the narrowest inverted "V" cut between the heel and sole to facilitate movement.

Comfort Before Style

The fashion for bulkier shoes was noted in Europe, but the U.S. was in the grip of another trend. The trade press reported: "the craze that swept America from coast to coast [was] a new shoe style with square toes and heels". In 1938, Ferragamo began exporting to America platforms with a solid cork sole for evening wear, . The sides of the platform gave him large areas to decorate, which he did either with Chinese motifs or hand embossing with brass and jewels.

Ferragamo's most famous shoe is probably a sandal that is said to have been created for Judy Garland. The platform and heel had layers of different colored suede and the upper was composed of padded gold kid straps. The sandal fastened around the ankle with a buckle. Heels had already reached 5 inch (13 cm), but Ferragamo was heading higher. High platform shoes might split in two, but wedges were stronger, so Ferragamo used the wedge . They were often cut into unusual shapes, aping modern sculpture. Ankle straps of all kinds came in and out of fashion, and high, thick heels and T-straps were features of the period.

Butterick Fashion Magazine of winter 1938-39 noted: "Daytime shoes have a bulkier, almost clumsy look... wedge heels, platform soles. Afternoon shoes retain some of their bulkiness... built up in front to give an unbroken line from toe to ankle." Although there was plenty of criticism about the look of these new styles, shoes had never been so comfortable. In women's footwear fashions, it is a rare moment when comfort comes before style.

A black patent leather mule (*right*), elevated on a sculptural wedge sole made from black laquered wood. It was created by New York designer Herbert Levine in the early 1960s.

Breathtakingly original de Haviland design with a heartstruck heel, from the 1997-8 collection.

Terry de Havilland

The 1970s British platform king Terry de Havilland used to have "Cobblers to the world" printed on his business card.

De Havilland went to work in his father's shoe factory in the East End of London when he left school. His father was a craftsman dedicated to making quality footwear. But in the early 1950s, he "got swept along with the tide of plastic rubbish, although he was never happy with it," de Havilland says.

In the 1960s, he took over his father's business and began producing a number of astonishing designs he later admitted he dreamed up, in the way of the times, while he was on acid. All the shoes he made had high heels. "I just can't imagine fancying a chick in flat shoes," he said. He made highheeled sneakers in violent yellows and purples; satin shoes that looked like bikini tops; sandals in fake zebra and ocelot skin, and thigh boots. But the de Havilland trademark was a tarty shoe in reptile skin with a platform sole, and staggeringly high heel.

De Havilland's platform(*right*) in suede with bead embroidery, is reminiscent of a Venetian style of the 1500s.

Across the Battle Lines

With the outbreak of the Second World War, it was no longer possible for women in Britain and America to buy Italian shoes, but fashion recognizes no battle lines. The corksoled platform shoe was worn by women on both sides. Lowheeled wedges, were also fashionable and even the clog made a comeback.

David Evins, the darling of American shoe design, created "clogs" for the exotic 1940s Brazilian movie star Carmen Miranda. The tiny South American Bombshell sent Evins back to the 16th-century chopine to create a visual balance between the outlandish gear she wore on her head and what she wore on her feet. Her rhinestone-encrusted wedges were sometimes 6 inches (15 cm) high. Pictures of Rita Hayworth wearing a pair of David Evins' satin slingback platforms with rhinestones around the sole were seen in many U.S. servicemen's lockers. The woman on the street, though, had to make do with plain cork wedges.

The wedge gradually fell out of fashion after the end of the war. There were many shortlived styles, like the Gondola, a shoe with a low wedge and a turnedup Turkish toe. Generally, a less bulbous style came in, but cork soles

Tiered wedge (*right*), in colored snakeskin by Terry De Havilland.

Lawler Duffy

Nicola Lawler and Laurie Duffy are part of the Brit pack of shoe designers who came out of Cordwainer's College, London, in the late 1980s. They made the shoes for couturier John Galliano's graduation show at St. Martin's College and have produced collections for designer Joe Casely-Hayford. In 1994, the Lawler Duffy design team combined two postwar fashion icons, wedges and blue denim, and came up with a range of sandals. They experimented with fish skin, and their shoes made in stingray hide and laminated salmon skin became very popular in Japan. However, during the early 1990s Duffy left the company and later, Nicola Lawler founded her Lawless brand.

Created in Canada in 1974, these silver platform shoes were designed for men, but women wore similar styles with high platforms, clumpy stacked leather heels and glittery fabrics. Rock stars of both sexes loved the style.

persisted on sandals. In 1949, wedges for men made a brief appearance. On 23 June, the *Shoe and Leather Record* announced: "London acclaims wedges for men. They are not new, John Winter & Son Ltd. has been making them for the past three years."

The Platform Revival

By the 1950s, the platform had given away under the onslaught of the Italian sandal and the stiletto. It remained out of fashion for 20 years until the platform revival of the 1970s took the 1940s fashion to even dizzier heights. Fashion designer Paloma Picasso claimed to have designed the first of the new wave in 1968, though Vivier made a platform sandal with an open toe and ankle straps in black-and-white Corfam, a synthetic material, in January 1967.

By 1968, the platform had reached London. Boutique owner Barbara Hulanicki designed a tight, suede platform boot with a 5 inch (13 cm) heel. Lines formed outside her trendsetting store Biba, in 1968 and more than 75,000 pairs were sold within a few months.

In 1969, a London shoe company, The Chelsea Cobbler, put a 1/2 in (1.5 cm) platform on a red, cross-strapped sandal. By January 1971, London's *Sunday Times* newspaper was reporting on "monster boots with vast club-like wedges, weighty legacies from the hideous Victoriana of Lancashire mills". The fashion was to get even more extreme and boots with shocking pink platform soles appeared. In July 1973, the *Observer reported*: "Down Kensington High Street, I saw a girl teetering on stiletto heels and platform soles. Crazy!"

The fashion also took off in America. One of the more inventive exponents of the platform was designer Henry Behar, who produced a range of outrageous rocking platform shoes from his New York basement in the 1970s. One white wooden creation had a round heel like a Life Saver (Polo) mint.

But an altogether plainer style was the real star performer of the 1970s in the U.S. The Kork-Ease was a 6 inch (15 cm) wedge sandal.

The rock star best known for his outrageous taste in footwear is Elton John. These boots, monogrammed "E J", were worn by him in 1973. A short man, he loves platform soles and stacked heels that give him a lift. These startling creations in silver leather have red and white leather stack platforms.

Made by Cherokee in Canada, these shoes have a scooped wedge silhouette that during the early 1970s was produced in every type of material imaginable.

The shoe with a stilted bamboo structure by Jan Jansen (*left*), led to a number of designs with PV-molded and bamboo soles.

The sole was covered in flesh-colored suede with vegetable-dyed waterbuffalo-hide straps fastened by a buckle. "Nobody actually designed them. We told the factory what we wanted and they made them," explained Sam Hersh, chief salesman of Julius and Sol Stern the company that marketed Kork-Ease from New York.

The Kork-Ease was successful because the insole molded itself to the wearer's foot, and the suede developed a rich, dark texture in use. They were reputed to be comfortable enough to wear in bed. The demand was so great that the company had to ration sales, but copies soon sprang up, some in flashy finishes. During the 1990s, several companies in the U.S. tried to revive the Kork-Ease.

Clogs, platforms, and wedges were the universal fashion among the young, including men, in 1975. At their zenith, soles were generally 2 inces (5 cm) thick and heels 5 inch (13 cm) high, although boots often had an additional lift inside. Some designers went to further extremes:

A platform sole and high heel in wood (*left*), produced in the 70s. The classic laced upper seems quite out of place on the extreme sole but was common at the time.

The pop star Madonna's platform shoes in maroon satin covered in sequinned stars (*below*). They were made in Italy by Dolce and Gabbana in the early 1990s.

Violet suede, Puritan-style platform shoes (*above*) by Canadian designer John Fluevog. Created in the early 1990s, they have the designer's "signature"—a distinctively flared heel.

Jansen gave the traditional Dutch clog a new look (*right*), but it was widely copied.

Jan Jansen

Although he is relatively unknown, Dutch shoe designer Jan Jansen is extraordinarily prolific. He has designed over 2,000 shoes, some selling tens of thousands of pairs around the world. But this success has also led to his designs being widely copied.

Jan Jansen was born in 1941 and started working in the shoe trade in Rome in 1962. In 1964, he began working under the Jeannot label and his ability to turn his prototypes into commercially acceptable shoes became legendary.

In 1969, he gave the Dutch clog a new look and created the "Woody," selling 100,000 pairs. But cheap copies from Italy began to swamp the Netherlands and Jansen was forced to abandon his creation.

Jansen had a huge success with an open platform sole made in cane at the *Semaine Internationale de Cuir* held in Versailles in 1973. The shoe gave the impression that the wearer was walking on air. But when Jansen began to manufacture it in Hong Kong the following year, he again found that it was being copied.

This prolific shoe designer created two collections a year which were made in Italy and sold through retail outlets all over the world. In addition, he produced four collections of unnamed designs a year for leading manufacturers, not only in the U.S., but also Brazil and Taiwan. In the early 1980s, he produced the Bruno range of shoes with a wedge hidden inside, made in combinations of leather, imitation animal skin, and patent leather. One of his best designs, which had a distinctive diagonal zipper, was copied on a large scale. A Dutch importer sold 400,000 copies on the home market, but the shoe was copied so exactly that Jansen was able to take legal action and successfully secured the right to sell the copies in his own shop.

In the early 1990s, he began producing work under his own name. This liberated him and he branched out into unconventional materials such as Plexiglass, bamboo, and cork. He used vivid colors with a palette of brilliant red, peacock blue, saffron yellow. The shape of his shoes is often extreme, not to say erotic, but they are wearable. Jansen is now recognized as one of the masters of the shoe world. Perhaps, at last, he will reap the rewards of his original and undeniable talents.

Sculptural and asymetrical style (*below*) epitomizes Jansen's original and eclectic ideas.

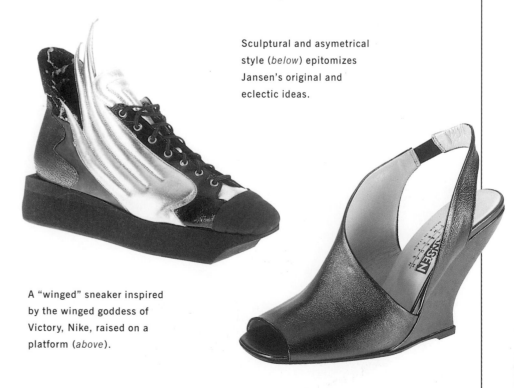

A "winged" sneaker inspired by the winged goddess of Victory, Nike, raised on a platform (*above*).

"Wet look", patent leather, and synthetics were the height of fashion in the early 1970s. These classic open-toed shoes, with platform soles and high heels, are from that period.

Rolando Segalin made a pair of satin boots with heels 8 inches (20 cm) high.

High wedge soles gradually took over from platforms. The wedge gave designers a larger area to decorate. In the mid 1970s, they used fluorescent colours and disco glitter, though Delman produced a wedge in plain cork. But by 1978, everyone had come down to earth again and the platform and wedge disappeared, leaving behind a low, sculpted form, rather like that displayed by a clog.

Retro Arrives

In the 1980s, Ralph Lauren experimented with a wooden platform with a black suede upper. Japanese designer Rei Kawakubo made a laceup clog with leather uppers and wooden soles for Comme des Garçons. But it was the retro revival in the early 1990s that brought platforms riding back on a wave of disco nostalgia. Dance floors were pounded by rhinestone-swirled platforms and high vinyl sneakers.

The much-derided Jesus sandal (*above*) could be given a spin that made it almost fashionable, just by adding a platform sole and working in sophisticated brown suede rather than leather.

Low-level black and white platform soles (*below* and *right*) are enlivened by colorful suede uppers seemingly fixed to the sole by a line of brass studs.

A selection of Prada platform shoes with ankle straps (*below*).

Brogues

Brogues are oxford-type shoes with a sturdy reputation. They are strong walking shoes that conjure up images of long country walks and robust rural pursuits. But on the feet of Fred Astaire or Gene Kelly, lighter versions appear to fly. The country associations that surround brogues to this day are rooted in history. The shoes originated in rural Scotland and Ireland. Initially they were heeless shoes, usually made of thick untanned cowhide and kept in place by laced thongs. Hay or straw was stuffed inside to prevent chafing. The holes punched in the uppers, which are now only for decoration, once performed a practical function by allowing the water drain out of the shoe as the wearer forded streams or clambered through bogs.

A spectator, or co-respondent, brogue in brown and cream leather by Nicklish French c. 1914. A popular style of shoe which makes a frequent re-appearance on the fashion scene. The classic brogue (*right*) by one of the masters of the shoemaker's craft, Lobbs of St. James, London.

A CHAP'S STURDY SHOE

Slowly the brogue developed into a sturdy shoe made of tanned leather rather than rawhide, and sewn with a horsehide thong. When heels were added later, they were made of tanners' leather shavings glued together and dried beside a fire. The finished shoe was rubbed with a rag steeped in melted candle wax to make it waterproof. An outer shawl tongue was added in about 1640, which was fringed to lend a touch of elegance. Over the years, two types of brogue developed: the "single" consisted simply of an upper and a sole, while the "double" had strip of leather or welt between the upper and the sole. Both are still in evidence today.

The pattern of punched holes in the uppers of a shoe is known as broguing. The classic brogue is an oxford (a lowheeled, laced shoe) with broguing on the toecap and around the serrated edges of the heel counters, the apron, and the overlaid panels. Broguing sometimes appears on ankle boots and women's day shoes too.

Another shoe grew up alongside the brogue. Known as the gillie, or ghillie, it was named after the guides who assisted the hunt in Scotland. The gillie differed from the brogue in that instead of lacing the shoe through eyelets, the lace passed through wide leather loops sewn to the quarters. When the loops were closed tight, they formed an extra layer over the tongue, making the shoe more waterproof. Today, gillie lacing is used on many different types of shoe.

History of Brogues

The modern brogue originated sometime between 1776 and 1789. It became popular following the development of a machine that could sew the uppers, patented by American Charles Weinenthal in 1789. During the 1860s, the Blake, an American sewing machine, was adapted to use waxed thread to sew the uppers to the soles, which was essential to keep the shoes waterproof.

In the 1700s, brogues became the standard footwear of working people in Scotland and Ireland. However, the gentry adopted them for hunting. The shoes were made from grainy leather with gimped

A catalog page showing a range of Goodyear-welted men's footwear at reasonable prices. They exhibit a variety of broguing and decorative edge techniques that remain popular.

A leather derby, manufactured in Switzerland c. 1916. The wing tip and quarter of this decorative shoe are decorated with broguing and silk ribbon lace.

Florsheim

"Son of a bitch. That was a goddamn Florsheim shoe," said Jack Nicholson in the movie *Chinatown* after half drowning in a reservoir and losing his shoe. Seconds later, his nose is split open, but he is definitely more upset by the loss of his shoe. In America, formal shoes *are* Florsheim. With around a quarter of the non-athletic shoe market, many people, from boxer Muhammad Ali to former president Richard Nixon, have been seen wearing Florsheims. The company was established in Chicago in 1892 by Sigmund and Milton Florsheim, who had emigrated from Germany. Since then, Florsheim has become as synonymous with the wingtipped brogue and the loafer as Nike is with the sneaker.

The company is not short of innovation. In 1996, it came up with a shoe they claimed never needed polishing. The leather was treated chemically so that the shoe was resistant to scuffs, water and watermarks. The company say the time saved shining works out at around ten minutes a day, that's eight hours a year and some 400 hours in a working career.

(serrated) edges, and ornamental punching in a variety of patterns. Brogues were usually brown, but in the Highlands of Scotland and in rural Ireland, upper-class women kept a pair of black brogues for dress-up wear.

By 1905, fashionable Scottish lairds were wearing brogues with a fringed tongue. The thongs that fastened the shoes ran through slots formed by turning the top edges of the leather under, in a refined form of gillie lacing. This made them more waterproof and the ideal shoes for country pursuits such as walking and hunting. Golfers added studs, and brogues were adopted as the classic style of shoe for this outdoor sport.

Street Style and Fashion Flair

The brogue also became fashionable as a street style. The fashion shoe was made in more refined leathers and had a less rugged silhouette. By 1920, a fringed and gimped tongue that covered the laces was added. The Prince of Wales, later King Edward VIII, was seen wearing them with a kilt, on his trips to Scotland. In the 1920s twotone styles became popular, particularly in the U.S. The toecap and quarters were in a dark color while the rest of the upper was lighter. These "spectators," known as

Shoes for dandies: decorative stained oxfords, c. 1920, with distinctive silk ribbon laces.

From Bally, 1936, a twotone brogue with calf saddle and unusual 'cut-outs.'

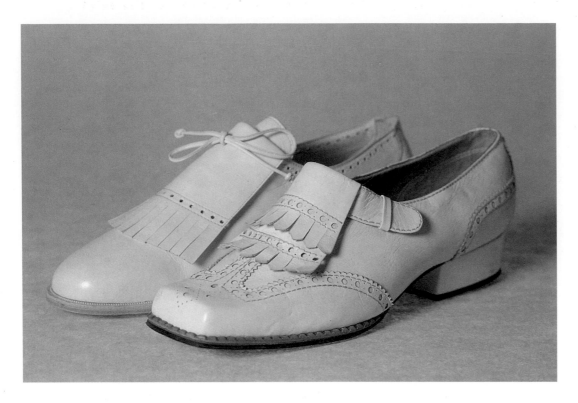

Shoes of 1968 and 1973, reflecting a "golf" styling. The "ghillie" tongue is trimmed and has a punched decortation. The low heel and broad toes are both very typical of the period.

co-respondent shoes in Britain, came in three different color combinations: a light creamy beige with a rich dark brown; black and white; and brown and white. They reached the height of popularity in the 1930s, though they continue to sell to this day. They had a great following in Hollywood. The tapdancing movie star Fred Astaire was particularly fond of them and championed a lightweight version of the two-tone brogue as a dancing shoe.

Broguing became so popular that it also appeared on derbys, boots, pumps, and mules. In 1966, strollers with broguing and serrated edges on both the vamp and the quarters appeared, as did gillies in brown, green, or blue calf, or suede.

During the 1970s, the fashion for maxi skirts brought with it higher heels. A narrow, gently rounded toe was needed to complement the look, and the shoes were decorated with broguing. The brogue became the most widely sought silhouette for women and came multistrapped, laced through eyelets, around hooks, or through gillie loops. The ends of the laces were often finished with decorative metal tags or beads. Brogues had become high fashion, and the style that had begun in the bogs of Ireland was now striding down the catwalks of the world.

In the 1970s, broguing returned to men's shoes, too. It gave a masculine look to the forepart of the shoe, offsetting the more feminine effect of the higher heels which had become fashionable for men. Even men's casual shoes were brogued around the topline and the wing tip. There were also twotone versions of these shoes.

An unusual "walking shoe" (*below*) by Bally c. 1941, with decorated platform and deep, rounded silhouette.

British Style

Today, the brogue is regarded the world over as a British style, particularly when made in brown leather. Indeed, some of the best exponents are found in the U.K.: Church's, Barker, Loakes, Grenson, , and Oliver Sweeny create made-to-measure brogues.

The shoe manufacturer Church's features broguing on nearly half its men's line, adding it on boots, buckled shoes, and tasseled loafers as well as ties, or laceups. Most of their oxfords feature extravagant swirls of broguing on the toecap. They produce traditional, single-colored and twotone brogued golfing shoes. One style, the Carnoustie Atlantis, is all white; others have gold studs on the sole. Despite this ornamentation, the company sets great store by the traditional

From 1928, a men's leather and canvas spectator (or co-respondent) derby, by Bally, c. 1928.

Lobb of St James's

If you want to spend over $1,600 (£1,000) on a pair of handmade shoes, go to St. James's Street in London and visit John Lobb, Bootmaker. Lobb is noted for its men's shoes, particularly brogues, oxfords, and loafers, which are hand sewn with twisted and waxed threads.

A pair of Lobb bespoke shoes can take up to six months to make and involves the skills of a number of craftsmen. First, the fitter measures the customer's foot, then a wooden last is carved by the lastmaker in beech, maple or fine hornbeam. The hide or skin is selected by the clicker (cutter). There are over 50 different types of leather to choose from, including calf, pig, deer, buck, lizard, elephant, ostrich and python. At least eight pieces of leather are used for each shoe and the clicker picks them individually for weight, color and grain. The leather is cut into the required shapes, stitched, and assembled by hand.

Lobb was founded in the mid 1800s by John Lobb, the son of a Cornish farmer. To raise the money to begin his business, he first went to Australia. There, his prospector's boot with a hollow heel in which miners could hide gold, was a great success. John Lobb returned to London and, in 1866, set up shop in St. James's Street and went on to become bootmaker to Edward VII. The firm has been in family hands ever since.

The company almost foundered in the Great Depression, and John Lobb's grandson Mr Eric, until then a farmer, took over in an attempt to save the company. He kept the shoe shop, by then a revered institution, going throughout the Second World War, even though it was bomb damaged six times. The only precaution taken was to move the lasts into the country for safety.

Today, Lobb's collection of lasts numbers over 30,000. They are stored in alphabetical order of customer on racks in the basement of the St. James's shop. Lobb also keeps another invaluable archive, *The Book of Famous Feet*, which contains penciled outlines of the feet of the company's most noteworthy customers. Lobb boots and shoes carried King Hussein of Jordan and Emperor Haile Selassie to their

Two classic toecapped brogues by Lobb, 1997. The shoes display the discreet punched patterns and understated styling of this master bootmakers. Right, the vast last store in Lobb's basement.

thrones, the Shah of Iran into exile, and Lord Louis Mountbatten to war.

In 1956, Lobb received its second royal warrant, when the company became bootmaker to the Duke of Edinburgh. The Queen's warrant followed in 1963, and the Prince of Wales' in 1980.

In 1987, Lobb won the French Craftsman of the World title, but Eric Lobb was already aware that royal patronage and prizes do not keep a company afloat. As early as the 1950s, he went to America to drum up trade. At one party in Boston he was asked to measure and make shoes for everyone present, Soon, Americans were making the trip to seek him out in. Lobb also courted the new aristocracy—pop stars such as Mick Jagger are clients.

Gucci

In the late 1970s and 80s, Guccci's double "G" logo spread across the world and was seen too much, but now the label is back at the height of upscale fashion.

Guccio Gucci (1881-1953) started a saddlery shop in Florence in 1906, after the family's millinery business failed. He made leather luggage, handbags, wallets, and purses.

A shortage of leather during the Second World War prompted Gucci to use canvas. It was then that he introduced the famous, bold red and green bands which became a trademark. In the 50s and 60s the company's products became the epitome of Italian quality and style and Jaqueline Onassis and Grace Kelly were among its clients.

By the late 1970s, more than 10,000 items, from coffee mugs to whiskey bottles, were franchised; the label was so ubiquitous that it became meaningless. After an number of boardroom disputes, Maurizio Gucci, grandson of the founder, called in Dawn Mello as Design Director from 1990 to 1991. In the reconstruction that followed, many franchises were closed and the double "G" was dropped from the outside of the company's products.

Mello put a team of designers to work on the Gucci archives. They resurrected old styles and gave them a new twist. Suddenly, the respectable Gucci loafer appeared in metallics, sherbert-colored suede, and satin with a rhinestone trim.

One of the young designers was Tom Ford, who created entirely new lines that were still recognizably Gucci. In 1993, Investcorp, who already owned half of Gucci's stock, bought Maurizio Gucci out and installed Ford as director of design. Gucci has not looked back since.

A fabric and tan leather tie shoe, made by Parlo Leoni for Volare, U.S., c. 1967-71. The shoe has the broad, soft, rounded toe so popular and widespread during this period.

construction of its shoes and their water repellence. The secret, it says, lies in the "Goodyear welt," invented by Charles Goodyear in 1872 and adopted by Church's soon after.

Waterproof Construction

The Goodyear welt construction is complicated, but essentially it puts an extra layer of leather between the foot and the ground. The insole of the shoe has a rib around the edge. The insole is tacked to the shoe last—a metal or wooden form—then the finished upper (the outers, linings, toe, and heel stiffeners) is pulled over the last and attached to the insole rib. Next, the welt, a strip of leather about ⅛ inch (4 mm) thick, is prepared and then stitched to the upper and the insole rib.

The stitching of the insole, welt, and upper leaves a hollow area under the insole that is filled with a mixture of cork and resin. This is designed to give the insole extra flexibility and allow it to mold to the shape of the wearer's foot. Finally, the outer sole is attached and twin-

A beautifully detailed glacé kid tie shoe by Herbert Levine, with decorated suede saddle, c. 1970.

Church's shoes: cottage industry to multinational

The family firm Church's, a maker of traditional British shoes, has expanded into the U.S, Canada, Europe, and the Far East. Worldwide it has some 160 stores and concessions in about 60 more.

Church's was founded in 1873 in Northampton, England by three brothers, Alfred, Thomas, and William Church, and it has stayed in family hands ever since. The current chairman, John Church, is the grandson of one of the founders.

During the 1800s the making of shoes had been a cottage industry and the cobblers worked in their homes. The three founding Church brothers had the idea of bringing all the skills of shoemaking together under one roof. The company now has three factories in the U.K. and one in Canada, and employs 2,000 people worldwide. Another factory in Italy produces a range of handmade moccasins exclusively for the company. The

Northampton factories alone produce over 5,000 pairs of men's shoes each week and Church's keep 50,000 pairs warehoused at any one time.

The key to Church's approach is the amount of time the company spends with its designers, range builders and licensees to ensure that the flavor of its collections is identifiably British. This close scrutiny does not mean that it make no changes. In the middle years of the 1990s, the company produced the Church 2000 brand, aimed at a younger market, who wanted a more flexible and casual approach to style. It also introduced the Classic Boat Shoe range for yachtsmen, which is now selling in 22 countries around the world.

Church's have always prided itself on its classic Goodyear welt method of production. However, this restricts the company's market, as only 6 percent of

the world's footwear production uses this method. Church's has now adopted modern methods and machinery and is tackling a larger market.

The company is also promoting its image and its name outside the area of wellmade footwear. It now sells silk ties, socks and belts under the Church's name. These are seen as particularly chic in Scandinavia.

A classic brogue derby in black calf.

Joan & David brogue for women in onyx and taupe calfskin (*above right*), and Bruno Magli with tapered toeline (*below*).

stitched to the welt with a tight-twist thread. Church's says this construction of its double brogues makes them "the shoes of kings."

Gatto, Rossetti and Florsheim

Although the brogue is associated with British shoemakers, the Italians also produce some of the most elegant brogues as fashion shoes. Founded in 1912, Gatto of Italy produces refined versions for its wealthy and exclusive clientele. In the 1990s, the company added a distinctive, subtle square toe to its collection. Fratelli Rossetti produces a line of spectator shoes for men and women known as sportivo.

In the U.S., Florsheim have been producing superb brogues for decades. They are made from leather that comes from a horse's hindquarters, known as shell cordovan hide. The leather is widely acknowledged as the best in the world for both its durability and looks. These handsewn shoes are worthy rivals for any British manufactured brogue.

The Ambassador Sport Oxford, Style No. 502
An unusually smart sport oxford in white Buckskin with tan trim. Also to be had with black trim. Style No. 503. Sold by a leading dealer near you. Ask for Style Booklet.

Johnson & Murphy produce shoes for presidents and gangsters alike. Frank "Lefty" Rosenthal (*above*), whose character is fictionalized in the 1995 movie *Casino*, favors a pitch heeled, patent leather design.

Johnston & Murphy

It is no secret that President Clinton is an Elvis fan. So when he ordered a pair of black captoe oxfords from the Nashville shoemakers Johnston & Murphy, the company sent the president a pair of blue suede penny loafers too.

Johnston & Murphy were not surprised that Bill Clinton wanted to wear its wing tips. Every president since Millard Filmore (1850-53) has worn its handcrafted shoes. The company was established in 1850 by English immigrant William J. Dudley who set up a shoe factory in Newark, New Jersey. Dudley teamed up with James Johnston in 1880 and built a reputation for making shoes of high quality. When Dudley died in 1882, William H. Murphy became Johnston's new partner and the company became Johnston & Murphy.

The company moved to Nashville, Tennessee, in 1957 and remains one of the few American firms that makes a line of shoes entirely by hand. Since 1948, this has been done under the auspices of Domenick DiMeola, who learnt his craft in Italy using tools inherited from his father and grandfather. In 1963, DiMeola recruited and trained Raymond Robinson, who is currently Johnston & Murphy's master craftsman. Robinson made Bill Clinton's blue suede shoes.

Bill Clinton was one of five

Three contemporary outdoor styles from Johnston & Murphy. From the left: saddle oxford in nubuk and waxy leather, with discreet punching; walled toe tie shoe in nubuk; tie boot with padded collar and understated decoration.

presidents to have selected captoe shoes from Johnston & Murphy. The list of presidential captoe wearers includes another distinguished Democrat, Harry S. Truman. According to the company's records, Bill Clinton, with size 13C, has the biggest feet of any president since Woodrow Wilson. Rutherford Hayes, with size seven, had the smallest. President Clinton wrote back: "I received your shoes and letter—my wife and I loved the blue suede shoes and were surprised to hear Woodrow Wilson had big feet." Although he has long been considered a rather boring president, Woodrow Wilson ordered far more exciting shoes from Johnston and Murphy than Bill Clinton. He ordered the same style, but in white buckskin.

Johnston & Murphy have a roving exhibition of presidential shoes. Twelve presidents' footwear is represented from Abraham Lincoln's black laceup chukkas to Ronald Reagan's classic Ambassador captoes. But the company could not find any of Ulysses S. Grant's shoes, so they put Grant's shoe lasts on display instead. Other presidents represented in the show are Chester A. Arthur, Woodrow

Wilson, Warring Harding, Dwight D. Eisenhower, John F. Kennedy, Lyndon Johnson, Harry Truman, Richard Nixon, and Gerald Ford.

Johnston & Murphy make shoes for mobsters as well at presidents. When movie director Martin Scorsese was making the 1995 movie *Casino*, based on a gangland feud in 1970s Las Vegas, he called on Johnson & Murphy. Scorsese had cast Robert DiNiro as Ace Rothstein, a character modeled on mobster Frank "Lefty" Rosenthal. Scorsese wanted absolute authenticity. A pair of Rosenthal's size 12A handmade shoes were sent to Johnston & Murphy to use as a model. The company made seven pairs of

A graceful advertisment from the 1930s extolling the virtues of the sturdy, wing-tip walking shoe, "in fine scotch calf skin."

high, pitched heel, patent leathers in light pink, gray, turquoise, royal blue, and beige for DiNiro's feet.

When Rosenthal himself saw the shoes, he immediately ordered several new pairs of Johnston & Murphy's for himself. He chose the same style, but otherwise his taste had sobered with the years. His new shoes were in black, burgundy, and midnight blue. Jack Nicklaus, Tommy Lasorda and Arnold Palmer also wear Johnston & Murphy shoes.

The black tie shoes made by Johnston & Murphy for Bill Clinton. The classic blue suede mocassin with traditional saddle, made expressly for President Clinton.

8

Loafers & Moccasins

The moccasin is the Native American's contribution to footwear. It was taken up by the early colonists and through them found its way back to the Old World, where it evolved into the very symbol of understated elegance, the Gucci loafer. The moccasin is essentially a leather bag for the foot. A single piece of hide wraps around the foot, forming the sole and the upper, though in many versions a second piece of hide is sewn in to form an apron that covers the top of the foot. The loafer is essentially a twopiece moccasin but has a hard sole and a strap or saddle, made of leather, over the instep. Expensive, upscale loafers retain the moccasin's tubular design in which the leather from the shoe's upper wraps under the foot. The design makes the shoe particularly comfortable. In cheaper styles of loafer, the leather upper is cut and sewn to the sole as in regular shoes. The name "loafer" probably comes from the German *landläufer* meaning a wanderer, or vagabond.

Three traditional moccasins (*above*) produced by North American Indians. Each one is made of soft leather, forming a bag around the foot, and has bead decoration. Two have leather thong ties. Derived from them is the modern loafer in leather (*opposite*).

SOFT-SOLED STYLE

Sperry Top-Sider

In 1935, an avid yachtsman named Paul Sperry had been working on developing a skid-resistant, rubber-soled shoe to wear on his yacht.

An idea came to him after examining the paws of his cocker spaniel, Prince. He noticed that the deep, wave-like grooves on the pads of its paws gave the dog its grip on the ground. Sperry reproduced this pattern in the crepe rubber soles of canvas sneakers and found that it gave him and his crew near-perfect adhesion on wet, slippery decks.

Soon after, he developed his first leather boat shoe, the "Top-Sider", as an alternative to his canvas original. Not only did the Top-Sider become standard equipment for yachtsmen and professional sailors around the world, it also evolved into a fashion item. In 1979, Sperry Top-Sider Incorporated was bought by The Stride-Rite Corporation, which has continued to expand the line.

The origin of the moccasin probably dates back at least 10,000 years. Moccasins are closely related to the ancient foot bags of Northern Europe and Asia, where primitive people simply wrapped a piece of hide around the foot and tied it at the ankle. The first people to arrive in America crossed from Asia to America by way of the land bridge that existed at the Bering Straits in the last Ice Age. At some point after they crossed, these early Native Americans began refining the idea of the foot bag. They used soft deerskin or tougher buffalo hide and molded it more closely to the shape of the foot. While Europeans developed hard soles for their shoes, Native North Americans did not. The soft sole gave the wearer greater stealth in hunting, was more practical for kneeling in canoes, and worked better with snow shoes.

The Algonquin tribe gave the moccasin its name; it is their word for a soft-soled shoe. The Algonquin and many other Native North American tribes decorated their moccasins with pieces of animal quill that they colored. When the Europeans arrived, beads superseded the quills. Women colonists, whose feet were constricted in tight, European shoes, quickly saw the advantages of moccasins and adopted the deerskin version for indoor wear. The all-American shoe was born. American frontiersmen adopted the more rugged buffalo hide version of the moccasin. The hide was a practical choice as it is resistant to wear and actually toughens with use.

Eventually, moccasins began to appear in Europe. On April 26, 1792, a Quebec housewife, Mrs. Simcoe, noted in her diary that although Indians did not come to town as often as they used to, she ordered some moccasins from them to send to her daughters in England. "Those I bespoke were to be much prettier colours [sic]. I think them pretty for little children in the house," she wrote. However, she saw the danger of the girls' feet spreading. "I should be afraid if the older one wore them,

The range of Sperry Top-Sider shoes evolved from the all-white yachting shoes (*left*) to leather lace-ups (*right*) that might more readily be seen on the High Street, worn by people who never set foot on a boat.

Advertisement for moccasin-style men's shoes in the Saturday Evening Post.

their feet might be too large ever to wear the Duchess of York's shoe." The then Duchess of York, Princess Frederica of Prussia, was known for her tiny feet. They were 5 7/8 inches (15 cm) long and just 2 inches (5 cm) wide at their widest point and were said to rival those of George Washington's wife Martha for daintiness.

The Construction

In the 1900s, moccasins, loafers and their derivatives have appeared in many forms. Some designers maintain the original design, some modify it, while others simply imitate the general look of the moccasin. But the range of styles, from classic penny loafers, to boat or deck shoes, rugged handsewns to driving shoes—the most recent addition to the family—is united by the construction.

The modern moccasin's most distinctive characteristic is the "U"-shaped apron. It is also the feature most commonly copied by its imitators. The top edges of the vamp are gathered and, usually, hand sewn to the "U"-shaped apron, or plug, as it is sometimes known, which covers the top of the foot.

The true moccasin, in which the vamp passes under and around the foot, forming both the bottom and the sides, has many advantages. Its unstructured nature allows it to form around the foot instead of squashing or constricting it. There are no hard edges and few seams, making the shoe extremely comfortable.

Making a moccasin is different from the manufacture of other shoes. The clicking, or cutting, of the leathers is a simpler process because the moccasin has so few pieces. The apron is sewn to the vamp by hand and the completed structure is forced on to the last. Sometimes the leather is shrunk to the shape of the last by wetting it and leaving it to dry on the last. In its modern form, the moccasin sometimes has an outer sole, which is lockstitched to the bottom part of the vamp.

The Norwegian Moccasin

The moccasin did not have much of a following at the turn of the century, but in the 1930s, when men's clothing became more easy and casual, the unlined Norwegian moccasin was popular, especially in America. By 1935, they were in mass production in Britain. The style had developed in Norway after early Norwegian explorers had brought moccasins back from North America. The Norwegian moccasin had a hard leather sole and a plain saddle. And, in what seemed like a revolution at the time,

A black calf leather, welted moccasin in a classic style that might be worn by men or women. This dateless favorite was made by Grosvenor.

Minnetonka Moccasins

Minnetonka Moccasins celebrated 50 years in business in 1996. The American company's initial success came in the 1960s when the moccasin became a favourite with hippies. In the 1970s, the company's Thunderbird beaded moccasin fed the urban cowboy craze and, in the 1980s, they led the fashion for driving moccasins. The company believes that, despite passing trends, the moccasin is in for the long haul. David Miller, Minnetonka president and the grandson of the company's founder Philip Miller, says: "We're sensitive when we come out with new things. We're more concerned with what we're selling, one year, two years and five years from now."

Bass Leavitt Penny Loafer

The Leavitt Penny loafer was named after Norm Leavitt, an employee of the Bass shoe company who worked in the firm's quality control department for 40 years. It was introduced in 1936 and retailed for just $8. The design was patented for 17 years, due to its flat, rather than beef-roll strap that held a coin. The line has continued in production and celebrity wearers include James Dean and Michael Jackson.

they were slip-ons. Their "U"-shaped aprons were influential and they began to appear on other shoes. The aprons were known as Norwegians, or skis.

The Sahara sandal was introduced for women in 1931 and reached a peak of popularity around 1933-35. Despite its name, it had a moccasin construction. The sole curved up around the edge of the foot and upper, but between the vamp and the quarter the sides were left open like a sandal. Sahara sandals were tied on to the foot by thongs.

Casual slipons, often with a moccasin-style apron front, were back in fashion in America by the 1950s. The 1947 Sears Catalog, offered a "teenwise slipon" for girls that was "as casual 'n' carefree as a coke session, as smooth as your pet date dress and simply 'out of this world' with your tailored sports togs or sweater 'n' skirt outfits". The upper was made of soft, vegetable-tanned leather with an antique finish to give it that "mellow, worn look you'd expect from any well-behaved slipon". Moccasins or loafers in antiqued brown calf became the fashion for school girls.

The Penny Loafer

One variety of loafer, known as Kerrybrooke Teenright Smoothies, had a good luck penny in the vamp saddle across the front of the shoe. The fashion for tucking a one-cent coin under the saddle so that it showed through a slot in the leather gave this slipon shoe the name penny loafer. In the 1950s loafers were taken up by the students at Ivy League colleges. The penny loafer was the most popular and was worn by both sexes. The Weejun, made by G.H. Bass, attained cult status among Ivy League students. In the 1990s G.H. Bass updated the Bass Weejun in brown leather. This new penny loafer put the penny back in a slot in the saddle. Even Chanel warmed to the idea, producing highheeled penny loafers for women. But, being Chanel, they had their own coins specially minted.

In the mid-1950s, Henri Bendal began importing Belgian loafers through his tiny store in midtown Manhattan. The line went on selling well for the next 40 years. The design of the handmade "moccasuals" was based on a Belgian felt peasant slipper. The Belgian loafer has a small wedge heel made in calf skin. The upper is outlined with piping and there is a small bow on the apron.

Over the years the colours and materials have changed. The Belgian loafer now comes in crushed velvet, suede, brocade, mock lizard, Belgian linen or patent leather. Bendal has had to change the name too, after copies began appearing around the mid-1990s. He now calls them Belgian casuals, but for devotees they will always be Belgian loafers. Each pair is handmade so they have to be ordered well in advance.

A pair of Sebago moccasins (*above*) made in the U.S. They have a composition sole but a leather upper with traditional leather thong laces and leather thonging around the sides of the ankle.

Made in 1947, this is a classic cream and navy loafer (*below*) with stitch welt and a stacked leather heel. The upper has a moccasin look to it.

A moccasin-look slip-on made by Bally in 1947. It is in tan suede with a decorative seam and lace.

Sebago

Sebago was founded in 1946 and made its first boating moccasin in 1948. With 800 employees the company produces between 35,000 and 38,000 pairs of up-to-the-minute designs and classic shoes a week. This is quite an achievement when each stitch is knotted individually in a way that cannot be duplicated by machines. The company's most famous shoe is the "Sebago Dockside" with its antislip sole, which was introduced in 1969, nearly 30 years later, the shoe is still in production.

But the wait does not dampen the enthusiasm of their fans as one customer said, "These are the only shoes I don't mind waiting two years for."

The loafer owes its popular image to the 1950s. In 1957, Elvis Presley was seen wearing white buckskin loafers in the film *Jailhouse Rock*. The style was particularly associated with the West Coast of America. In his 1958 novel *Playback*, Raymond Chandler wrote of one character: "He was California from the tips of his port-wine loafers to the buttoned and tieless brown and yellow check shirt."

Italian manufacturers added interwoven leather uppers to the loafer to make the shoe cooler in summer. According to the Sunday Times of 1966, Gucci's shoe, with its miniature gilt stirrups, had become a "status symbol accessory". The Gucci moccasin had originally been introduced in 1957, as a man's shoe in brown or black leather. It is a tubular loafer and the upper part is one piece of leather which completely cradles the foot. The famous gilt snaffle-bit was soon gracing the feet of Clarke Gable, John Wayne and, later, Grace Kelly and Audrey Hepburn. Other manufacturers of loafers quickly picked up on the snaffle Gucci had added to the saddle of loafers, and added all manner of little gold chains to their own. In 1972 tassels were added to shoes that fashion writers described as "upscale loafers".

Native North American Revival

In 1973, Native North Americans seized the old battleground of Wounded Knee and tried to repossess the moccasin too. A new awareness of their heritage led tribal craftsmen to update their designs for the modern world. The updated Cree moccasin was made of moosehide and the cuff around the ankle was lined to help it stand up and to show off the patterns of beading that decorated the exterior. The bead pattern continued down the tongue and apron as far as the toe, reducing the puckers around the seam.

The modern Winnebago moccasin was more widespread. The large tongue was lightly beaded and the cuff was folded and stitched to form a tube for the lace thong. By 1980 loafers were being worn by both sexes, they went well with the baggy jeans fashionable at the time. Weejuns stayed in style in Ivy League colleges until the fashion for Timberland boots came in. And, despite its many imitators, the black leather Gucci loafer continued to be a status symbol. Jealously guarding its green and red canvas ribbon held to the saddle by gilt horse buckles, it still oozed the effortless arrogance of Old World money. In 1989, Gucci introduced a women's version with a low, stacked heel in a range of leathers and colors. But the snaffle-bit motif remained, even on the satin version, as a reminder that the house of Gucci was begun by the Florentine saddler Guccio Gucci.

However, loafers began to be rivaled by the new driving shoes designed by Diego Della Valle. Inspired by the non-slip driving shoes worn by European sports car drivers, Della Valle came up

The shoes in brown suede (*below*) were made in the late 1950s for the singer, Buddy Holly. The low cut is similar to a moccasin, though the buckle is a departure.

continued page 102

Patrick Cox

Once seen as the enfant terrible of the shoe world, Patrick Cox is now a revered establishment figure. His shoes are chic and his ideas are as copied as those of Gucci or Chanel. But it is hardly surprising that the creator of the Wannabe is himself surrounded by wannabes.

Lively Patrick Cox designs from the 1990s featuring multistriped leather in rainbow colors to create eyecatching effects on traditionally styled shoes.

A design from the 1990s. This is a brown calf-leather moccasin with a traditional penny loafer saddle.

Patrick Cox was born in Edmonton, Canada in 1963. He abandoned his childhood ambition to be a doctor when he discovered the night clubs of Toronto. His club dress made such an impact that Loucas, a local fashion designer, hired him to oversee the style of his shows.

Cox began by firing a young, then unknown model called Linda Evangelista, but he made better judgments over shoes to go with Loucas's collection. Unable to find what he wanted in Canada, he customized some Kung Fu slippers from Toronto's Chinatown. Loucas liked the result and suggested Cox go to London and study shoe design at Cordwainers College. At the time, Cox was obsessed with everything British: it was the the 1980s, the New Romantic era, and Cox read the cult magazine *The Face* and worshipped

Vivienne Westwood. Shortly after enrolling at Cordwainers he had the good fortune to get to know one of Westwood's assistants, who let slip that Vivienne desperately need new shoes for her forthcoming show. Cox seized his opportunity and sneaked three pairs he had designed into the models' dressing room on the day of the show. At the time, Westwood was passionately against platform shoes. But the models liked Cox's shoes, so Westwood let them wear the giant gold platforms with gold knotted vamps. Cox's cheekiness paid off, he had been noticed, and his shoes went on to become a staple feature of Westwood's shows.

When he graduated from Cordwainers in 1985, he had a dozen pairs of shoes, enough to exhibit at the London Fashion Week. Over the next three years, he made shoes for designers Katherine Hamnett,

Richard James, John Galliano, John Rocha and Anna Sui. Unfortunately, however, his financial turnover remained low.

Cox did not want to be a cult London shoe designer, who achieved much press coverage, but did not make any money. Gucci and Prada are his role models and he is more interested in being a businessman and designer, than merely a designer. He also had production problems, he either made his shoes in London's sweat shops, where both the quality and delivery were erratic, or he went to shoe factories in the leathermaking town of Northampton where his men's line in black, brown and white could be produced but not the more innovative designs.

In 1988, Cox found a factory in Italy that was able to give him the quality and the flexibility he needed. Unfortunately, he had to give his old suppliers six months' notice, and the following season he went bankrupt because he had no shoes to deliver. Once he started to manufacture in Italy his business picked up and his designs became more disciplined with a consistent look. In a short time he had more than 50 stockists in Japan, Europe and America.

In September 1991, Cox opened his own shop in London. The following March he created the "Wannabe", a line of chunky loafers in brightly colored leather. No sooner had the shoe gone on sale, than other companies started copying it. Cox turned the situation to his advantage; and hired the factory in Italy that was making the best copies to make his originals. Sales of 10,000 pairs were expected in the first season but hit 20,000, and long queues formed outside his London shop.

In July 1994, Cox opened a branch in Paris, and in March the following year he opened his third store on New York's Madison Avenue. By Fall 1996, he had sold one million pairs of Wannabe shoes, and has now launched a range of Wannabe clothes, Patrick Cox bags, wallets, and a collection of tennis shoes called PCs.

A black leather moccasin (*below right*) with a plain apron.

A moccasin (*left*) in gray tweedy fabric with black calf-leather trimmings.

A Wannabe loafer (*right*) in bright reddish-brown crocodile-look leather with a large silver buckle. Wannabes first appeared in 1992.

A well-made brown leather moccasin (*left*) with a two-tone leather saddle.

Catskill Mountain Moccasins

President and founder of Catskill Mountain Moccasins Mark Goldfarb lives in a cottage in Woodstock, New York, but sold his store there in 1993 to travel around craft fairs and music festivals selling his wares with his wife and co-worker Diane. Making moccasins has allowed them to live where they want and still do their work. It took Goldfarb 14 years to get to that point but by 1994, his solely owned venture Catskill Mountain Moccasins was churning out between 1,000 and 1,200 pairs a year and making $2 million (£1,850,000) gross.

Goldfarb has plans to expand into wholesale and is exploring the idea of producing a video catalog. But he will have to iron out the problem of foot sizes because he is used to making each pair of moccasins individually to a cast of the clients foot. "If you say make me a size nine, I don't know what you mean," says Goldfarb. Nevertheless, the business continues to expand.

Four square-toed moccasins by Emma Hope (*above*) from her "Regalia for Feet" range. They are in velvet, suede and crocodile leather.

with the J.P. Tod range in 1979. The basic design is a unisex moccasin with small rubber studs embedded in the sole. The shoes are light, flexible and comfortable, and now come in more than 150 styles and 100 colors.

Boat Shoes

In 1996, the boat shoe was given a revamp by the Americans Sebago and Sperry. They abandoned the traditional brown and replaced it with black or white patent leather for street wear. Yachtsman Paul Sperry also added a patent leather sole, but he added his distinctive wavelike grooves so that the shoe would grip on a wet deck.

The real hero of the 1990s loafer is the London-based designer Patrick Cox with his "Wannabe" range. Cox exaggerated the features of the standard loafer, raising them up the ankle, enlarging the tassel, broadening the saddle, giving them stacked heels and even decorating the aprons with Union Jacks. Presented in soft, padded leathers, Cox's Wannabes have been an international success story.

In America, the home of the moccasin, the tradition continues. Florsheim make classic loafers and moccasins. The jewel in the Florsheim crown is the Yuma, a traditional moccasin based on a Native American design. Fashion pundits call it a "fuss free loafer in the Prada mold," but Florsheim have been making them unchanged for 70 years now.

The company Catskill Mountain Moccasins produces lowcut moccasins with prices

A pair of tan leather moccasins (*above*) by Dooney & Bourke. They have leather laces and simulated tightening thongs at the sides.

starting around $270 (£169). For $3,000 (£1,875) you get an elaborately decorated, five-button boot version. Based in Woodstock, New York, Catskill Mountain Moccasins have satellite workshops at Dallas, Texas; Taos, New Mexico; Westfield, North Carolina; and Redding, California. Nine moccasin makers design and handstitch the silhouettes. Each averages 10 orders a day.

Although they use many traditional techniques, the soles of Catskills moccasins are hightech. They can be customized with polyurethane soles, Vibram-cushioned running soles or spikeless golf shoe soles. They come with sheepskin footbeds, and with uppers in American buffalo, shrunken bull hide and Scandinavian elk.

The moccasin is made to measure and the process begins with a soft cast made by surrounding the stockinged foot with gaffer tape. A last is made from the resulting mold and the shoe is created inside out in the stitch-and-turn tradition. The leather is usually colored and decorated with beadwork and a choice of buttons that are either turquoise-studded sterling, antler or British halfpennies. Clients include singers Joni Mitchell and Lenny Kravitz.

A pair of moccasins in dark brown leather with a decorated saddle, and heel pulls. They were designed by Joan & David.

Three very chiseled moccasins (*left*) in thin, lightweight leather by Katharine Hamnett, each with a gold trim on the saddle.

Three suede moccasins which are updated "Hush Puppies", designed to be worn by men or women. The one below, in a color called "top brass", has the HP logo on the saddle.

A pair of dress moccasins with a high, straight heel. They were designed by Katharine Hamnett and made in London.

103

9

Boots

There is an essential paradox about boots. Their original design was staidly functional for use out of doors on route-marches, but they quickly became fashion items which have been, and still are, worn well outside the practical context for which they were first intended. The boot is basically a shoe with a "leg" that rises, at the very least, to the ankle, but which sometimes climbs to the knee and can even extend halfway up the thigh. Its history has always been linked to the military, and in fact the evolution of the boot can be traced right back to the Roman legions. As Roman soldiers marched northwards into Europe they were forced to abandon their Mediterranean sandals for an enclosed shoe to keep their feet warm.

Julius Caesar, conqueror of Britain and Gaul, was reputed to have worn a pair of boots made of solid gold. Equally sought after by the young "warriors" of the 90s is the Cat Boot. This is a design which brought what were once hiking boots on to the city streets.

A pair of boots by the French bootmaker Pinet (*above*), dating from the period 1878-1985. They are decorated with an embroidered floral design and silk rosette at the top and were undoubtedly intended to be worn by a lady as evening wear. By contrast, the Cat boot (*opposite*) from the 1990s is a rugged boot for men in waxy leather with a padded collar and heavy cleated sole.

U.S. soldiers riding on the cowcatcher of a train on an expedition to Mexico in 1916. The kneelength boots worn by cowboys and cavalry officers, and even the heavy boots worn by infantry soldiers were to become cult items later in the century.

MADE FOR WALKING

A soldier in shoes is only a soldier, but in boots he becomes a warrior," said the Second World War hero General George "Old Blood and Guts" Patton. Soldiers' boots are also immensely practical footwear. They keep out the mud of the battlefield and help to protect the feet from injury and infection. They also protected the calves of the cavalry man and helped him to control his horse, while the foot soldier, too, drew comfort from the fact that his feet were warm and protected.

Well-shod feet can make all the difference in a battle. Napoleon dressed his troops in shiny boots that looked impressive on parade, while the Duke of Wellington took great pains to make sure his men were shod for the battlefield. Wellington also gave his name to a leather cavalry boot. It was not until this century that the Wellington boot was manufactured in rubber. The contrast in approach to boots can be seen again in the Second World War, when Adolf Hitler wanted his men goosestepping in shiny jackboots while the Western Allies wore solid, but practical, ankle boots.

Work boots are designed for the job. The boots of the coalminer or laborer are rugged and functional. Originally, they were made from the sturdiest leather with thick toecaps for protection. Later, the toecaps were reinforced with steel. Tough workmen's boots evolved into the western footsoldier's army boot in the 1800s.

The Riding Boot

In town, gentlemen of the 1800s did not need stout walking boots as they rode everywhere, and their boots had high heels to grip the stirrups. The boots reached the knee and protected the calf from chafing against the horses' flanks. Soft leather gave the rider more contact with, and therefore more control over, his horse. Tall boots also protected the rider from mud kicked up by the horse and from the weather. From the 1500s until after the First World War, riding boots were a major indicator of social status in Europe. In the 1600s, gentlemen's riding boots were made of soft leather and elaborately decorated, with patterns cut in the uppers, turnovers of fine lace or intricately sculpted leather, and extra side panels of leather. The tops were sometimes turned down, with a panel of a second color under a scalloped trim. More often the inside of the boot was a different color. This is the origin of the brown tops seen on black riding boots today. Waxed leather boots, more rugged and practical

These American men's ankle boots (*above*) date from 1915 but would not be out of place in today's shoe stores. They have a welted sole and a fabric trim around the ankle, heel, and lacing.

Images from a catalog of the Charles Williams Stores in New York City (*opposite*). These calf-length men's storm boots are made from calf elskin, from moose and from kangaroo grain, with a full bellows tongue.

Highly decorated calf-length cowboy boots (*this page and opposite*) in various styles popularized by the artists and followers of American Country music.

El Presidente

The American craze for cowboy boots even reached the White House. President Harry Truman set the trend when he ordered a pair from bootmaker Tony Lama in El Paso, Texas, who called the design "El Presidente". Dwight D. Eisenhower and Lyndon Johnson, who were both Texans, and later, Jimmy Carter and Ronald Reagan all followed in his footsteps and wore cowboy boots regularly.

than their forebears, were introduced in the 1700s. From the mid-to-late-1800s, boots became less popular in civilian life as riding became less of a necessity, but in the military they continued to be seen as a mark of rank. During the First World War, British officers wore calflength riding boots while the lower ranks wore anklelength laceups. As the use of the horse declined and armies became more democratic, generals adopted the same footwear as their men. However, some armies continue to wear high leather boots, particularly for ceremonial parades.

The Cowboy Boot

One type of riding boot has risen to prominence on and off the horse—the cowboy boot. The original cowboys of the mid 1800s wore any type of boot or shoe they could find, but toward the end of the frontier era, they adopted the U.S. trooper's boot. Later, a modified version of the footwear worn by Mexican cowboys, or vaqueros was adopted. For better control in the saddle, the shoe part of the boot fitted tightly. This, and the sloping heel which gripped the stirrup, made them difficult to walk in but excellent for control when riding.

After the Civil War, cowboys began to adopt lowheeled, hightopped boots made in a hard, black leather called kip. These were often made by German immigrants who based their designs on Northern European riding boots. The most popular was the Coffeyville Boot, made in Coffeyville, Kansas. It combined elements of various U.S. cavalry styles and the original British, leather Wellington boot.

By the end of the 1860s, highheeled boots called saddle dandies had taken over.

Ruth Roland, the queen of the silent westerns, had a pair of boots with scalloped collars inlaid with tiny flowers that topped columns of intricate fleur-de-lis patterns. They were made by C.H. Hyer & Sons in Olathe, Kansas, whose 1925 catalog features a pair of boots with huge eagles with outspread wings, clutching red, white, and blue shields in its talons front and back. The eagles have three, white stars over their heads that stretch up to the perforated, white collar.

The fashion for increasingly exotic cowboy boots peaked in the mid 50s. The state of the art was probably reached in 1955, when *The Cattleman* magazine reported:

"Last summer a customer wearing handmade boots walked into the John Furback jewelry store in Amarillo, Texas and asked to see their silver belt buckles. The jeweler could not concentrate on the sale for staring at the customer's boots. His practiced eye skipped over the richly engraved, sterling silver plates covering his boot heels and toes. Right in the middle of the toecaps were mounted two-carat diamonds.

'Sir,' John Furback, Jr., asked the stranger, 'would you mind showing me your boot tops?'

The man obligingly peeled up his trouser leg. In the middle of his cordovan boot top was the emblem of the state of Texas embroidered in pure gold thread, complete with the blazing lone star".

Heel heights reached an upper limit of about 4 inches (10 cm). The back of the heel sloped gently until the sole was no bigger than a quarter. Drover, Stovepipe, and Cattleman models were popular, the legs of these boots were at least 14 inches (35cm), and many boots were thighlength.

Until 1900, cowboy boots were plain. In 1903, the first embroidered toe wrinkles—lines of stitching across the top of the toe—appeared, and cutout leather designs, often in a star pattern, were sometimes overlaid around the collars of the boot tops.

Boots for Movies

Early cowboy movies were made in the Eastern States and exaggerated costume styles were based on illustrations in cheap novels and comics, and the cowboy shows of the vaudeville entertainer Buffalo Bill. Actors, such as Edwin S. Porter, star of the 1903 movie The Great Train Robbery, and Billy Anderson, wore oversized bandannas and heavy chaps of sheepskin or leather, covered with metal studs.

In about 1914, the movie industry moved to California and employed real cowboys wearing their own clothes. But the authentic clothes looked dull, so the cowboy actors tucked their trousers inside their boots to show off the stitched boot tops. Tom Mix, the biggest cowboy star of the 1920s, pioneered the heavily embroidered cowboy shirt and the boots to go with it, with inlaid leather designs and many rows of stitching. The 1923 catalog for the Justin Boot Company in Forth Worth, Texas, boasted a Tom Mix boot with black kangarooskin vamps and kidskin legs inlaid with white tulips.

The Italian shoe designer, Salvatore Ferragamo, set up his shoemaking business in Hollywood in 1923. He came to Cecil B. de Mille's attention when he made the boots for one of the producer's westerns. "The West would have been conquered earlier, if they had had boots like these," de Mille said.

By the 1920s the Old West was long dead, but in 1926 the Dude Ranchers'

A French designed boot (*right*) by Andrea Pfister from the 1992–93 Winter Collections which, with its cuban heel and mid-calf length, takes its inspiration from the cowboy boot—in gold kidskin with multicolored suede inlays.

Two highly decorated, calf-length cowboy boots (*above*)—designs are tooled into the leather and often use contrasting colors to make them more eye-catching.

Association was formed which provided ranch holidays for city dwellers and a lucrative new market. By the 1930s, C.H. Hyer & Sons of Olanthe, Kansas was offering boots with leather inlays depicting steer heads, stars, half moons, dice, diamonds, initials, ranch brands, hearts and butterflies. In response to this competition, the movie stars' boots became even more kitsch. The singing cowboy Gene Autry began wearing boots with narrow, square toes covered in long, perforated wing tips, which are the ornamental toe covering of the boot. These contrasted with the rest of the vamp and were matched by the foxing (reinforcement) around the counter. The legs were inlaid with tall, multicolored flowers and leaves that surrounded a white longhorn steer's head in leather. The finishing touch was provided by silver spurs and buckles.

In the 30s and 40s, bootmakers vied to outdo each other with colored leathers, stitching, and exotic materials, decorating their boots with decks of cards, oil derricks, spiders' webs, prickly pear cacti, and bucking broncos. Throughout the West, new bootmakers sprang up selling through stores and mailorder catalogs, with cowboy boots for men, women, and children.

Europe also found itself in the thrall of the cowboy boot. Paris couturier Jacques

Fath visited Texas in 1949. He ordered cowboy outfits for himself and his wife, held a square dance in his chateau the following summer, and introduced his interpretation of cowboy style in his couture collection of August 1950. Other Parisian couture houses quickly caught on and cowboy boots made in leather, suede, and even satin appeared.

In the 1960s, the myth of the cowboy began to undergo some revision and in the southwest of the U.S. there was an economic upswing. Conservative Texans needed more sober boots to wear with their Brooks Brothers suits, and inlaid designs and complex stitching were replaced such as sharkskin, ostrich, lizard, and snake. Lower heels were required for businessmen more likely to be driving a Cadillac than breaking a mustang.

City Styles

Women came into the 1900s wearing boots. Lower class women wore anklelength boots that laced severely up the front. Stout, everyday boots were made in leather. Upper class women wore luxurious, glossy glacé kid boots. A popular design had a black patent leather shoe with leg in black cloth. Brocade, velvet and antelope skin were worn by more flamboyant souls on special occasions. The boots had small, fairly thin heels, that were either shaped like a pedestal or straight. Women also wore buttoned boots with kid or cloth legs, scalloped along the buttoned edge. Eighteen-button ladies' boots were still being made in the U.S. as late as 1925, they were difficult to fasten and a buttonhook was essential to do them up.

In the early part of the century some boot styles were remarkably unisex. Both men and women adopted the hightopped Balmoral boot which buttoned to one side. Often known simply as bals, they were made with a galosh, or shoe part, of patent or glacé leather, and legs of cloth or matte leather. Winston Churchill was a devotee and was photographed wearing bals with cloth tops from 1908 to 1916 and with matte leather legs from 1913 to 1929. Another wearer was Charlie Chaplin who favored black patent bals with beige cloth legs. This twotone effect was developed from the turn of the century into the 1930s, when it gave way to shoes and spats. The effect was much the same but, being detachable, spats were easier to clean.

In the early part of the century, men also wore high derby boots which laced up the front. They were also remarkably similar to women's boots of the same period and continued to be popular into the 1930s. There were boots with elastic sides too, but they temporarily went out of fashion in the 1920s.

Two pairs of high-heeled, lace-up ladies' boots from the early 1900s. The pair (*above top*), made in 1914, are American-designed and are a smart, more tailored version of elaborate "Gaiety Girl" styles. The shiny pair (*above bottom*) are beautifully made in glacé kid, created in 1917 in Canada.

The "Balmoral" boot (*right*) was named after Queen Victoria's castle in Scotland and was popularized by her consort, Prince Albert. This version has a fabric spat with a button fastening above a foot in shiny black leather. The style was worn by both men and women in the late 1800s and early 1900s.

Very closely fitted to the leg, these English-made boots (*right*) from around 1915 are in a sleek style with a high heel and a scalloped topline. A button hook would have been needed to fasten all the tiny buttons.

Buttoned from toe to knee, this magnificent pair of high-heeled, gold embossed boots (*above*) would have been custom-made for a lady to fit her legs perfectly. They were made in Sweden around the turn of the century.

Russian Boots

Women's buttoned boots were replaced by Russian boots, which were straight topped, kneehigh leather Wellington boots, with a pointed toe and a Louis heel. In May 1921, The British Shoeman magazine remarked: "The picturesque Russian boots in suede and leather caused quite a sensation at the Grand National meeting."

In December 1925, another trade paper, the Footwear Organiser reported: "The extraordinary demand for Russian boots has spread all over the country. It was first seen in May 1921... a few more each winter." By 1927, the magazine reported that "the smarter type of highlegged boot, close fitting to the leg" had a zipper. A rubber version was developed by the British company Dunlop. They came in brown with a pointed toecap and a 1½ inch (4cm) Cuban heel, but these "wellingtons", as they came to be known in Britain, were rapidly relegated to the feet of ardent gardeners and those who liked to tramp across the fields on wet days.

Fashion boots went into abeyance as civilian wear during the 1930s. From 1930 to the mid 1950s, they were associated in the public's mind with Fascism, Nazism, and war. Boots became the exclusive preserve of soldiers. The only other places a leather boot could be worn were on horseback, or on the sports field, though the inoffensive ,rubber Wellington boot trudged on.

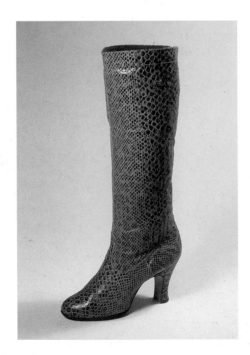

A knee-length, high-heeled ladies' boot in black and brown snakeskin. It was made in 1926 by Swiss company Bally. It seems likely that it had a zip fastening at the back.

White leather ankle boots (*left*) with the button fastenings that were popular from the late 1800s on into the 1920s. Called the Diamond shoe, this pair was made by Canadian company Queen Alexandra Shoes in 1916, and is notable for a sturdy "bulldog" toe.

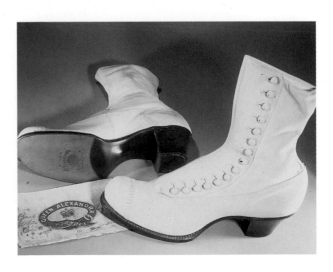

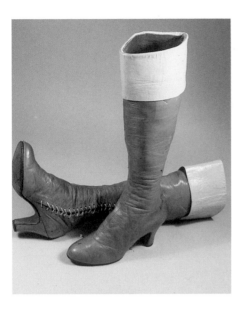

Two very different pairs of French fashion boots. The knee boots (*far left*) are a Russian-inspired design in teal blue and cream kid leather, created by Perugia in 1925. The shocking pink party boots (*near left*) take their inspiration from Greco-Roman sandals but have a delicate bow, trimmed with a marquisite buckle. They were made by Greco around 1920.

In the late 1950s, shoes began to creep up the ankle again. They were associated with sports and the upcoming generation of peacetime youth, rather than war. First came the soft canvas basketball boot. Next came the inoffensive desert boot. This was a soft suede version of the polo chukka boot that rose to the ankle and was closed with a lace through two eyelets.

With the arrival of the 1960s, fashion moved on fast, especially in Britain. First came the Chelsea boot, which had elastic sides. It was an updated version of the 1900s Chelsea that had first appeared as a riding boot. The elastic meant the foot could come free from the boot easily, preventing unnecessary injury if a rider were thrown. But the new boots were fashion accessories, not functional footwear. In September 1960, "new versions of the chukka and Chelsea" were announced by the U.K. shoe trade, which "give that long lean look that goes with the latest types of trousers [pants]".

Swinging Sixties

In London, the fashions of the "swinging Sixties" began by borrowing heavily on the past. But a unique style of the time soon developed. The roundtoed Chelsea boot sported either stylish pointed toes known as winklepickers, or square, chisel toes. The

American-designed "tango" boots (*below*) from the 1930s. They were worn for the newly fashionable dance craze of the period. This pair are in black kid leather with steel beads.

Twotone leather boots (*above*) with a sunray pattern on the toecaps and a checked pattern around the ankles. The sunray was a popular Art Deco motif in the 1920s. This pair was made in England in the early 1920s.

Mid-calf length boots (*below*) were fashionable during the 1960s. This one, produced by Bally, is in red velvet with the buttons, trimming and foot in black calfskin.

celebrated pop group The Beatles added Cuban heels and, in 1964, took them to America where they became known as Beatle boots. Later, zippers were added as the leg became longer.

In the 1960s, much of women's fashion was also dictated by Britain. On 4 September 1960, the Observer newspaper had already noted the boom in leather knee boots for the young of both sexes. "The craze for girls' boots was encouraged by Brigitte Bardot," the newspaper said. "With very high heels, [they] make girls feel bigger and more confident." The ankle boot of the late 1800s made a comeback in 1961 and was worn with jeans or pants. Boots became universal in 1962 and, in 1963, they went thighhigh—though they were "neither a fetish nor waterproof," the Manufacturers' Association warned.

The Go-Go Boot

But the calflength "go-go" boot was the design of the decade. They were brash and shiny, usually in black or white, or a combination, and made in vinyl. They were unabashedly sexy and were worn by miniskirted girls. Reaching to the knee, they concentrated the observer's attention on the thigh. The more adventurous the girl, the higher the boot, and thus the higher the focus of attention. Emphasizing their sexual connotations, boots that came up to the midthigh were known as "kinky" boots. The nomenclature was typically 1960s. Since such high boots were bound to

Two ankle boots from Italian designer Ferragamo. The 1930s, black suede boot (*above*) with the rhino horn toe has a silken, tassel-ended laces. The boot (*left*) is in gold brocade, and designed for evening wear.

have kinks in them, it allayed the suspicions of the staid older generation. But to young people "kinky" meant sexual deviant. Sex sirens wore them with stiletto heels, and they came in leather and suede in a myriad of colors. Even transparent plastic and silver foil space suit versions were designed.

The designer Courrèges made some impact with his space boots in 1964. These were flatheeled, fastened with Velcro, and they had square or peep toes. Other soft ankle boots relied on bright fabrics for their impact. Towards the end of the 1960s, the laced ankle boot of the 1900s made a comeback as the granny boot which accompanied the shortlived fashion for maxi skirts. However, nothing could rival the ascendancy of the go-go boot. As the decade wore on they were made in soft, stretchy fabrics that clung to the leg. Leather versions came with zippers. Then, in the 1970s, when platform soles came in, the go-go boot simply raised itself off the ground 2 inches (5cm). In those androgynous days, the Glam-rock stars Elton John, Gary Glitter and David Bowie would not have appeared in public without their zippered, gold or silver glitter boots with 4 inch (10cm) stacks.

With the oil crisis of the mid-1970s and the resulting world recession, boots came down to earth again. Punk entrepreneur Malcolm McLaren and designer Vivienne Westward opened a shop called Sex in London's World's End and sold bondage boots, and punk footwear began to sport unnecessary zippers and metal toe caps.

The Dr. Marten, which began life as a comfortable walking boot, became

A 1950s calf-length boot, designed by Magli, in simple, twotone colors of beige and cream, with a beautifully, scalloped edging on a beige-buttoned fastening.

A white satin and silver kid ankle boot (*right*), with the tiny kitten heel which was worn by young, fashionable girls in the 1950s and 1960s. This boot was made by Bally in 1961.

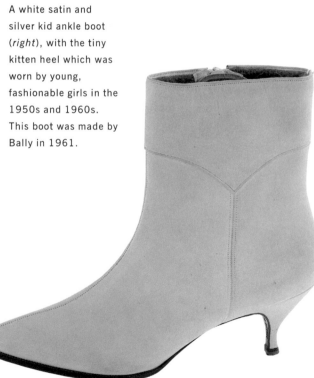

An ankle boot (*above*) in cream calf leather with a wool lining, made by Bally in 1962. The tiny stiletto heel and elongated toe were adopted by all fashion-conscious women at the time.

Known as the "Granny boot" because it had an Edwardian feel with its tight lacing all the way up the instep, this ankle boot (*right*) was made in 1961 by Bally. It is in black suede with black patent leather toe, heel and lacing.

115

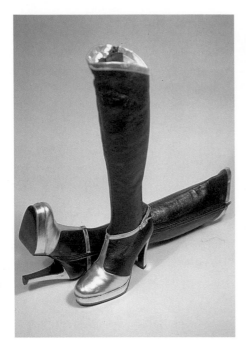

It was picked up in the thigh-high "moc croc" boots (*left*) designed by Herbert Levine in the U.S. in 1967. The black and silver kid boots (*far left*) are a 1970s slant-topped boot by Fox and Fluevog of Canada.

fashionable footwear in the 1980s. First manufactured in Germany in 1947, the "Doc Marten" was taken up by British skinheads and neofascists in the 1970s. By the 1980s the boots had made the transition to the catwalk and the pages of international fashion magazines.

Boots of the Ecowarrior

The American response to the "Doc Marten" was Timberland. The Timberland boot was the inspiration of Herman and Sidney Swartz. Their father, Nathan Swartz, owned the Abingdon Shoe Company in Newmarket, New Hampshire, and his two sons joined the firm in the 1950s. Abingdon produced work boots for other companies who marketed them as their own. In the 1970s, the business began to flag as their clients began to manufacture their boots in the Far East. The Swartz brothers decided that to save their business they would have to market their own product.

They hit the market with perfect timing. They tapped into America's growing nostalgia for its pioneer past and the growing interest in ecology. Timberland boots took the wearer into the great outdoors. As the Green movement spread around the world, so did Timberland boots, and sales soared. They were a fashion statement of the late 1980s and early 1990s. There is nothing aggressive about Timberland. They are the boots of the person who wants to be at peace with nature. They are the boots of the ecowarrior.

In formal wear, minimalist black nylon boots came into fashion in the 1990s. They were anklelength and understated, but boots cannot be kept down. By the middle of the decade, the British designer Vivienne Westwood was showing 1960s go-go boots in lurid colours. They quickly became popular and by 1997, kneelength boots with platform soles, last seen circa 1975, were in every shoe store.

A black, leather "biker" boot (*left*) from The Boot Store, U.K.—this is definitely a "no nonsense" type boot with its two strap fastening and simple, sturdy design. Timberland, tan nubuck boot (*right*) with black padded collar, natural, heavily cleated sole and striped laces—one of the original trendsetters for the hugely popular "hikey-boot" followers.

Biker's Boots

In the 1950s, boots underwent another radical change. From the late 1800s to the mid-1950s, the cowboy had been seen as the epitome of the existential outsider. But then the biker took over as the new symbol of rebellion. In the 1954 movie The Wild One, Marlon Brando wore heavy, lowheeled bikers' boots. And, like movie cowboys before him, he wore blue jeans with the legs turned up so that the upper part of the boot could be admired. These boots had returned to their functional roots. They were high enough to protect the biker's ankle from the heat of the engine and the exhaust pipe, and they had thick soles to protect the rider's foot, which was often trailed along the road while making a turn. It is notable that Brando's boots did have a solitary adornment—a strap fastened with a buckle across the top of the instep, which was curiously reminiscent of the straps used to secure spurs.

The strap appears again on the boots of Peter Fonda in the 1969 film Easy Rider. But Fonda wore cowboy boots, complete with high heels to grip the foot pedals of his Harley Davidson. The 1960s were generally a bad time for the cowboy boot. Influenced by the new fashions coming in from swinging Britain, they tried to adopt the British Mod style. One manufacturer even produced a cowboy boot in paisley patterned nylon—it was a disaster!

A Return to the West

It was 1975 before cowboy boots became fashionable again. New York fashion photographer Juli Buie, a native Texan, began to use them in fashion shoots, and wear them herself. Soon her friends were asking her to get pairs for them and she began to freight them across from Texas. In 1977, she put on a show at the Lone Star Cafe, on Fifth Avenue. Friends and celebrities modeled the boots—New York City Ballet star Jacques d'Ambroise wore his costume from Stars and Stripes, dancing to a cowboy band. Choreographer and tap dancer Tommy Tune could not fit his boots on his feet, so walked with them on his hands, and a top model stole the show, wearing white ostrich leather boots and chiffon and feather dress by designer Giorgio Sant'Angelo.

The slant-topped ankle boot (*above*), designed by Mary Quant in 1966, set a trend which spread to much taller boots—examples of which can be seen on the previous page.

Boots with gigantic platform soles and heels swept the fashion world in the 1970s, and were worn by men and women. This pair (*right*), with appliqué designs, were made in 1973 by Master John of Canada.

These knee boots (*above*) in black suede and gold kid were created by Yves St Laurent in 1976. He designed them to be worn with his Russian-inspired "Cossack" collection of clothes, and they were widely copied in the 1970s and 1980s.

Dr Martens

The most famous boot of all times, with its air-cushioned sole, millions of pairs of Dr Martens have been sold worldwide, and continue to sell. Both practical and fashionable, this boot remains one of the most "cult" styles ever invented.

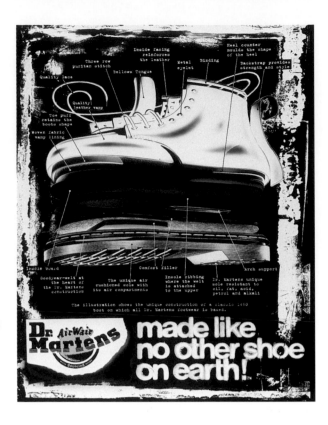

Dr Klaus Maertens, the inventor of the Dr Martens air-cushioned soles, 1960.

Dr Martens footwear is tough, with a sole resistant to oil, fat, acid, and petrol. They are sensible enough to be the type of shoe your mother would have approved of for school—well, almost. Instead they became the footwear of the rock world, a symbol of individuality and youthful rebellion, and an extraordinary phenomenon of fashion.

The classic Dr Martens boot—a black leather, 8-eyelet, lace-up with the original air cushion sole—started life as an orthopedic boot, was adopted by a military and industrial bootmakers in Britain, and emerged as an enduring icon of late 1900s fashion and the world's top, non-athletic footwear brand.

The concept for the patented sole was developed during World War II in a village near Munich in Germany, by Dr Klaus Maertens—who had injured his foot in a skiing accident and needed comfortable footwear—and his engineer friend Dr. Herbert Funck. The sole was known as Dr Maertens' air cushion sole. Over the next decade or so, footwear with this sole was produced for a small, highly specialized orthopedic market.

In the late 1950s, the doctors, looking to commercialize their idea, began discussions with British company, R. Griggs & Co. Griggs had begun as village bootmakers in Northamptonshire, England, at the turn of the century, and had built up a steady business in workwear and military boots. Increased competition in the 1950s, led them to look at ways of improving their boots. Griggs married their bootmaking experience to the orthopedic footwear with its air cushion sole, anglicized the name to Dr Martens, and on 1st April 1960, produced the first pair of Dr Martens boots, named 1460 after the date. Business increased steadily in the 1960s—at a time when demand for military boots was falling with the demise of National Service in the UK. But during the 1970s the boots became established as the footwear of rock musicians, an emblem of punk, rock, gothic and a myriad of other youth cultures. According to Griggs, the adoption of the brand by the bands came first, and they literally jumped on the bandwagon, and began to hone their

An advertisement (*left*) for "Doc Martens"—showing the mechanics of its unique design and famous, air-cushioned sole diagrammatically.

An advertisement (*right*) demonstrating how this marvellous invention—the air-cushioned sole—can be put into practice on the street.

marketing strategy afterwards. They repackaged the boot's industrial and military origins to target the young and fashion-conscious consumer with a rebellious, aggressive edge. Now the brand is distributed in over seventy countries worldwide, and around eleven million pairs are made every year.

The original "DM" 1460 boot, with its 8 eyelets, and the related 3-eyelet shoe are the basis for the ultimate in cool footwear for the streetwise and fashion-conscious. The range now includes sandals, brogues, loafers, and children's styles. All have the distinctive welted construction and come in many colors.

The distinctive "DMs" sole pattern is readily identifiable and Dr Martens footwear has a number of distinctive features. Z welt footwear has yellow welt stitching, and grooves running around the side of the two-tone sole like those on an old-time vinyl record.

Internationally, the brand is protected from counterfeiting and legal action has been taken to protect the reputation of this quintessentially English brand. This legal protection appears to be working because, so far, the design of the "Doc Marten" has never been "copied" by any one competitor—and remains one of the most unique boots ever invented.

The classic design (*left*) with yellow, stitched welt, cushion sole and high, ankle-laced styling on a round, heavy toe.

Juli Buie then began having boots made up by the Dixon's workshop in Wichita Falls, Texas. Then one day, in the early 80s, while driving near the Oklahoma border, she stopped at the old Olsen-Stelzer company in Henrietta, Texas—the company was just throwing out some unsold 1950s classic boots in lavender, orange, pink and pale green, so she bought all forty-four pairs and took them back to New York.

In 1982, Andy Warhol bought a pair and they became the fashion item of the season. Within weeks the Olsen-Stelzer rejects sold out. Juli took them as the inspiration for her own line of boots. She began making decorative and exotic cowboy boots: lavender boots with red wing tips and beige diamond inlays; black calfskin boots with white foxing around the counter and perforated wing tips that flowed all the way round to the side seam; solid red calfskin boots with huge red and black butterfly inlays; and boots in kelly green and mustard yellow with lavender counter foxing.

She sold this colorful collection from a second floor store called Texas on Manhattan's Upper East Side, next to boutiques that imported Italian suits and French silk shirts. Despite the Willie Nelson tapes she played, Juli found her clients

A short "trouser" boot (*left*) from Magli, in black patent leather with a silver metal vamp trim, versions of which decorated thousands of boots and shoes during 1996.

A 1997 design (*right*) by Joan & David. This is an updated version of the lace-up, Edwardian city boot. It is in mahogany brown calfskin with broguing and a high veneered leather heel.

Knee-length boots (*above*) in black patent leather, designed by Gucci and made in the U.S.

A high-heeled ankle boot (*left*) in shimmering satin, created by Joan & David in 1997 and christened "Think brown". Recently introduced, stretch fabrics have given a new sophistication to boots.

An open-toed silver boot by de Havilland with a front zip. It has an iridescent lining with a circular pattern that is picked up in the platform soles and heels.

Fem-Dom rules in these black, bondage, platform-soled boots which have black "spikes" up the zippered instep.

A knee boot (*right*) in bright tan leather with an unusual red heel. This 1997 design by Magli of Italy has a straight heel and a walled square toe.

This 1997 design by Dooney and Bourke is a mocassin version of an ankle boot. Lighter styling has taken over at the end of the decade.

were Japanese businessmen and Wall Street investment analysts and the boot boom was on again. In 1982, 17 million pairs of cowboy boots were manufactured in the US. Few, if any, were sold to cowboys. By 1985, however, the market in New York was saturated, so Juli Buie moved herself and her store out to Aspen, Colorado. In the late 1980s, U.S. sales slumped to about 8 million pairs a year, but by 1990 they had climbed again to 12 million a year.

In the 1990s, cowboy boots began to appear in the pages of Vogue and Harper's Bazaar. Elizabeth Taylor wore a pair to her last wedding and couturiers such as Jean Paul Gaultier, Alexander Julian, Georges Marciano and Ralph Lauren started making them. Every boot produced is very different from the boots real cowboys wore on the range. They are now a fashion icon with a style direction of their own.

An elegant city style ankle boot in two-tone suede with a zip fastening. This 1997 design by Magli is usually worn with pants or the longer skirt length.

Functional & Cult

It is the fate of most popular shoes to begin purely as a covering or protection for the feet and to end up as a fashion statement—some examples where this has happened are far more glaring than others. How many people who wear tennis or running shoes actually go jogging? In his seminal work *The Naked Ape* Desmond Morris points out that successive fashions in menswear always begin as sports clothes. A man, he says, can show off his status if he wears sports clothes while others are dressed more conventionally, provided he can get away with it. Both the top hat and the bowler hat were originally worn for fox hunting,

as was the tail coat. In the 1700s and 1800s, riding clothes had an impact on fashion in general. Today, it is basketball shirts, football sweaters, and sweat suits that influence everyday footwear. Other shoes succeed by simply being outrageous. Initially, their impact and influence far exceed their limited availability—until they are propelled to cult status among the gurus of style.

The glamorous and the functional—clear vinyl sandals (*above*), made in the 1950s by Edouards of New York for Joan Crawford, the sexy Hollywood film star. See-through materials have frequently been used to allow the bare foot to be seen. A pair of trainers (*right*) which may be used for sport but are more likely to be comfortable, leisurewear shoes.

Cool Comfort for the Hottest Contest—Another Exclusive Improvement in ALL STAR Basketball Shoes—"They BREATHE with every step you take!"

Demonstrating "breathing" action of AIR-FLO INSOLE

IMPROVED
ALL STAR
BASKETBALL SHOES

with the New
AIR-FLO INSOLE

They're Cool!

Another Exclusive Improvement by
Converse

Your Feet Deserve the Best—Wear ALL STARS

Basketball shoes with a high supportive ankle have been around for a long time, and have been worn both for sport and leisure. This advertisement highlights a design improvement—the air-flo insole—so the shoes "breathe with every step you take".

A very smart pair of shoes(*below*) for ten-pin bowling, with leather uppers in red, black and white. Shoes like this were worn only indoors and had soles that would not mark the bowling lanes.

PUMPING IT UP

This century has witnessed the relentless rise of the sports shoe. The trend began in the 1800s with the development of the sneaker and plimsoll. In 1832, in New York, Wait Webster patented a process whereby rubber soles could be attached to shoes or boots. By the 1860s, a croquet sandal was being marketed with a rubber sole and a canvas upper fastened by laces. The rubber soles meant the wearer could move about silently; as a result, the shoes became associated with sneak thieves and were known as "sneakers".

In the U.K., the New Liverpool Rubber Company developed a similar rubber-soled, canvas sports shoe. It was called the plimsoll because the line of rubber used to seal the join between the sole and the upper looked like the load-regulating plimsoll line on the side of a ship.

By the turn of the century, sneakers and plimsolls were widely worn by children and, when tennis became so popular in the 1920s, adults also adopted them. The 1930s brought a craze for health and fitness and sneakers became ubiquitous for sports and leisure activities.

In the 1950s, the "sneaker" became a symbol of youthful rebellion. The movie star, James Dean wore them both on and off screen, and early rock-and-roll fans wore sneakers with their "bobby sox". But in menswear, the sneaker was overtaken by the basketball boot which had the same basic design, but came higher up the ankle.

It is such a good-looking shoe that it is easy to see why the Converse All Star basketball shoe (*above*) became popular, first with players and later as a fashion accessory. Known as "Chucks", they were promoted initially by ex-player Chuck Taylor, whose signature appears on the

All Star Sneakers

The first "All Star" basketball sneaker, with a top that came above the ankle was made by the North Carolina shoe company Converse in 1917, but was largely overlooked at first. The man who launched it on the basketball community was Chuck Taylor who played for the Buffalo Germans and the Akron Firestones. In 1921, he was looking for a job when he wandered into Converse's Chicago sales office. With his evident powers of persuasion and his love of basketball, Taylor seemed the perfect person to market All Stars.

Once hired, he took them on the road. He drove across America, visiting small towns, conducting basketball clinics in schools and colleges, and selling the shoes by spreading the word about their comfort and performance. Taylor's feedback also led to a slight restyling of the original All Star. The sole was given a better grip and made sturdier to cope better with the wear and tear of the basketball court. The ankle support was also strengthened. Taylor's name became so closely associated with the redesigned All Star that, in 1923, his signature was added to the ankle patch and they were nicknamed Chucks. It was the first time a player had endorsed a sports shoe. In 1936, the Converse design became the official shoe of the U.S. Basketball Team.

In the 1950s, the All Star basketball boot became a fashion item. Mick Jagger was wearing a pair when he married Bianca, and Woody Allen took Betty Ford to the ballet in a pair of hightops. It is said that Bruce Springsteen owns twenty eight pairs of Chucks. In 1963, they were immortalized by artist Claes Oldenburg in his pop art sculpture Giant Gym Shoes, which featured a huge pair of All Stars made in wire, cloth, and painted plaster.

In the late 1960s, California surfers wore black lowtops with no socks. These All Stars were cut low round the ankle. In the 1980s, New Yorkers wore different colored Chucks on each foot—there were over fifty colors to choose from. Chucks were the fashion on the West Coast in 1982 with the Sean Penn movie Fast Times at Ridgemont High when they became the shoe choice for surfers and skaters. Since then, they have become available in some 200 varieties, including pigskin, corduroy, black velvet and suede.

Over 500 million pairs of All Stars have been sold. Half of the 10 million pairs made each year at Converse's Lumberton, North Carolina, factory are shipped overseas. Some 93 percent of Americans own at least one pair, and one in ten of them wears All Stars every day.

Running Shoes

In the 1920s, Adolf Dassler and his brother Rudolf began making running shoes in Germany. By the 1936 Berlin Olympics, they were top in their field. Their shoes had strips of leather added to the upper for support. The strips were the key to the

continued page 128

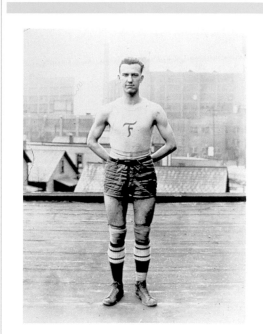

Running shoe wars

At the 1996 Olympics in Atlanta, Georgia, the battle between the manufacturers of hi-tech running shoes was at its height. Reebok was the official footwear supplier to the Olympic Games, but other companies launched massive promotions.

Nike attempted to promote its logo before the global audience. Some called it ambush advertising, but Nike called it fair game. The Atlanta Committee for the Olympic Games (ACOG) did not agree—and they forced Nike to remove its logo from track and field sportswear kits and even carried out an investigation of Nike's web site.

125

The "Green Flash" plimsoll (*left*) from Dunlop—a popular tennis and school games shoe in the 70s and early 80s—attempted a comeback in the mid 90s.

Training Shoes

Tennis shoes and running shoes are now all about technology. Manufacturers compete with each other over the latest hi-tech development. These shoes are no longer worn only for sports, they have become a street cult. To the streetwise wearer the right label and the latest gimmickry is as important as the newest computer game or the words to the latest rap track.

Trainers like these Adidas Campus running shoes (*above*) were fashionable in the 1970s and 1980s.

A Fila training shoe from their 1997 range, made of fabric with leather trimmings and a man-made sole. Shoes like this are generally designed by product developers who look at what the shoe is supposed to do and match appropriate materials and design features to create a shoe that will do the job.

Although the craze for tennis shoes seems to have begun in American, some British fashion gurus challenge that idea. The trend, they say, did not start on the feet of the joggers who sweated their way around American cities in the 1980s, but in Britain's soccer stadiums in the late 1970s.

In Liverpool, in the 1978-79 soccer season, trend-setting fans wore Adidas Sambas. When Puma brought out the Argentina and the Menotti styles, the fans quickly took them up. Adidas tennis and running shoes and Pumas were made in Germany and were not available in the U.K. at that time. But the overseas matches of these soccer clubs gave the fans ample opportunity to keep up with the latest continental sports footwear.

Enterprising individuals began importing them and, through soccer fans, the trend for wearing tennis shoes spread like wildfire across Britain and became ubiquitous in the inner cities. Eventually, they turned up on the feet of Mick Jagger and David Bowie on the video of *Dancing in the Street*. And that, some say, is how cult tennis shoes arrived in America.

There may be some truth in the theory, many footwear fashions do cross the Atlantic on the feet of pop stars, but the tale overlooks the history of Nike. The American company's roots go back to 1967 when Bill Bowerman, co-founder of the company began to develop the Marathon running shoe.

The first model to be released under the Nike name was a soccer shoe launched in 1971. It was named Nike after the Greek goddess of victory. Later that year came the first Nike tennis shoe, with its famous waffle sole of ribbed squares that gripped the ground. Bowerman made the prototypes of the sole at home by heating rubber in a waffle iron. In 1973, the U.S. track athlete Steve Profontaine became the first major track sportsman to wear Nikes, and Olympian athlete Jon Anderson and top tennis player Ilie Nastase followed suit. The next year, tennis star, Jimmy Connors, won Wimbledon and the U.S. Open wearing Nike tennis shoes. Nike kept expanding and in 1978, another player, John McEnroe signed an endorsement with the company. But more importantly for the tennis shoe fan on the American street, the Nike-Air basketball shoe, the "Air Force 1", was launched. In 1985, a promising basketball rookie, Michael Jordan, at the Chicago Bulls, endorsed Nike and the celebrated "Air Jordan" was born.

By then, Adidas and Puma were also making inroads in the U.S. Eddie Murphy wore Adidas trainers in *Beverly Hills Cop* and Puma were seen on the feet of the dancers in the Broadway hit, *A Chorus Line*. Fila of Italy moved into the market too.

Reebok, who had become trendy through the U.S. women's aerobics market, began marketing their tennis shoes solely as fashion items. The company produced the Noboks in 1996, it had a high heel and was not designed for running.

The tennis shoe has influenced

"Spitfire" from Fila's summer 1997 range (*above*). The track shoe has become an important part of street wear—proving that looking good does matters.

other types of footwear. Some manufacturers have pared away the uppers of tennis shoe designs and created sandals. Hiking, camping and other outdoor boots are also produced in styles based on the tennis shoe. There has even been a retro backlash when the U.K. company Dunlop attempted a comeback for its famous "Green Flash" plimsolls. This has encouraged other companies to seek design inspiration in past styles and Pods, Vans, Nose, Kickers and Campers are some of the 90s' most successful brands.

Chic women have also been seen in tennis shoes, although the extreme versions are far too bulky to be worn with stylish clothes.

A red and white suede plimsoll (*left*) by Puma (*left*), which was a simpler, less chunky forerunner of today's popular street styles.

Classically simple shoes by Roots of Canada. Made in 1980, these were some of the first shoes promoted with an ecological awareness. Since then, many shoemakers have marketed themselves as ecofriendly and environmentally conscious.

Elton John's Pinball Wizard boots

In the 1975 movie *Tommy*, based on rock musician Pete Townsend's 1969 album, Elton John played the Pinball Wizard. Director Ken Russell dressed him in massive Dr. Marten-style boots. Elton John said he would only play the part on the condition that he could keep the outsized boots. In 1988, John put on a sale of his rock memorabilia at Sotheby's. The boots were bought by the managing director of Dr. Martens. The international success of *Tommy* and Elton John's Pinball Wizard boots are some of the things that helped make the "DM" a cult item.

Well worn Union Jack shoes made by Dr. Martens in 1989. They produced many variations on the theme.

strength of the shoes. The first three-strip shoe—the origin of the modern running shoe—appeared in 1949. But then the Dassler brothers fell out and the company split. Adolf, known as Adi, went on to form Adidas, while Rudolf founded Puma. The two companies have been deadly rivals ever since.

The company, Reebok also began its life making running shoes—founded in 1895 in Bolton, Lancashire, Reebok made the shoes for Lord Burghley in the 1924 Olympics—and since featured in the movie *Chariots of Fire*. In 1982, Reebok was looking for a new market, when its Los Angeles salesperson spotted that women in aerobics classes were wearing versions of men's sports shoes in pastel colors. No company was designing sports shoes specifically for women, so Reebok introduced new styles in softer leathers with less rigid construction.

During recent Olympic Games, shoe stores have been stacked with products of non-sponsors covered in Olympic icons. The situation was so extreme that the ACOG turned to consumers and asked them to report violations. It ran advertisements in national magazines with the tag line: "How do you feel about cheating in the Olympic Games?" It also threatened to run the name and telephone number of the chairman of any company caught ambushing so that complainers could speak to them directly.

The Dr. Marten Cult

The cult shoe of the 1970s was the Dr. Marten. Dr Klaus Maertens of Munich began making boots with air-cushioned soles in 1945, after breaking a foot in a skiing accident. He started to produce his comfortable walking boots commercially in 1947. In 1960, the British footwear manufacturer Bill Griggs persuaded the German parent company to let him manufacture workmen's boots with a similar sole in Northampton, England, and the Dr. Marten, or "DM", was born.

In Britain, DMs were adopted as uniform wear by the police, postal workers and other public service employees. They were subsequently worn by skinheads who called them bovver boots, as they were useful weapons in street gang fights. Dr. Martens rapidly gained an aggressive image, in 1971, they were seen on the feet of violent, young thugs in

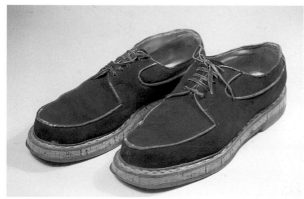

These blue suede shoes (*right*) pre-date Elvis Presley (who sang on the subject). They are from Frankfurt, Germany, 1948, and have cork soles.

rapidly gained an aggressive image. In 1971, they were seen on the feet of violent, young thugs in Stanley Kubrick's movie—*A Clockwork Orange.*

The boots became part of the uniform of the international, skinhead movement and were worn by young neofascists. But their aggressive image transcended these vicious associations. Gay men took to wearing "Doc Martens", partly for protection and partly as a gesture of assertiveness.

Women picked up on the "DM's" assertive image, too. At first, they were worn by hardline feminists, along with jeans and dungarees. By 1986, they were gracing the pages of Vogue and young women took to wearing them with chic and even sexy dresses, almost as a political statement. "DMs" had become one more weapon in the sex war.

The British shoe manufacturers, Clarks, persisted with the desert boot style (*above*), and helped bring them back to cult status.

The Desert Boot

The bland suede chukka boot was the male fashion statement of the early 1960s. It reappeared as a cult shoe in the mid-1990s worn by British pop stars such as Liam Gallagher of Oasis, Jarvis Cocker of Pulp, and the veteran Paul Weller. Desert boots were modeled on the boots worn by British officers in the North African Desert Campaign in World War II. They were introduced to the civilian market in 1948 by Nick Clark of the British shoe company Clarks. In the early 1960s, they were briefly taken up by the Mods, but were generally seen as too suburban and middle class to

Modern Hush Puppies (*below*) in bright two-color styles, designed to be worn by both men and women.

An early Hush Puppy advert (*left*), establishing it as a "leisure" shoe and linking it with the lovable dog that became its trademark.

They don't eat shoes, do they?

In the caring, sharing 90s, people converted to vegetarianism and strict vegans boycotted leather products. It was then that small, specialist footwear firms developed cruelty-free alternatives. Mocatan produced loafers, Chelsea boots and DMs in a fabric which is claimed not only to resemble leather and suede but allows the skin to breathe too. Clients include Julie Christie, Toyah Wilcox and Linda and Paul McCartney.

The very height of fashion in 1980. Brown leather clogs with wooden soles and uppers that have a "hand-stitched" look.

they had sold over 10 million pairs.

Desert boots were taken up by Paris couturier Karl Lagerfeld in the 1990s, he softened the look of his new military-style suits with twotone desert boots and many variations followed. Top shoe designer Manolo Blahnik produced a tobacco-colored version, while Nicole Farhi made them in a simulated ponyskin. Meanwhile, shoe retailers have gone back to basics, producing a number of square-toed styles based on the sturdier kind of chukka boot worn by polo players in the 1950s.

Hush Puppies

Although they were a popular success when first introduced in the 1950s, by 1993, Hush Puppies were seen as dreary. Clever product placement, however, has improved their outdated image. Hush Puppies began their new rise to stardom in 1994 on the feet of Forrest Gump, the anti-hero of the eponymous movie. U.S. fashion designers Anna Sui and Gene Meyer took them up and they soon appeared on the feet of Sharon Stone and David Bowie. In the late 1990s even that doyen of shoe fashion, rock rebel

Cult sandals varied from the unfashionable "Jesus creepers" (*above*) to designer flip-flops (*below*).

Fashionable, open-toed slingback sandals in red and black by DKNY.

The original Scholl exercise sandal (*below*) which was popular in the 1960s and 1970s. It had a wooden sole contoured to the foot, and was held on by an adjustable, leather strap.

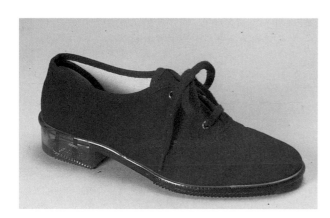

The Jazz Oxford, made in Canada in 1980, revolutionized the shoe business with its see-through plastic sole.

Liam Gallagher of Oasis has been seen wearing them.

The company concede that part of the Hush Puppies' new cult status is down to the retro look. But they have also had a major redesign with new styles and colors. Fashion designer, Paul Smith, was called in by the company to guide the brand forward, with the hope of making Hush Puppies rival "Doc" Martens in cult status.

Ecco, the Retro Cult Shoe

In the 1990s, the outdoor shoe of the 1970s, the Ecco, is also making a comeback as a retro cult shoe. The original Ecco was a straightforward, black leather, welted oxford with heavy stitching. Although they were originally designed as sturdy outdoor shoes, they have made the transition to office wear for those in the creative industries, particularly in the U.S. The transition was partly because the Danish firm that make them had taken the extraordinary step of producing a number of poetic booklets explaining the culture and concepts behind the shoe. The company's founder, Karl Toonsbury, has filled them with aphorisms such as: "A person spends an average of thirty years of his life in shoes. That time must be well-spent." These are shoes with added philosophy.

Green Shoes for the 90s

In the 1990s, young people became more conscious of ecology and the need for conservation, and a new American company called Deja Shoe began making the world's first commercially produced, recycled shoes. Called variously, Eco Sneaks and Envirolites they incorporate a diverse range of recycled materials. The foam used in the tongue, for instance, is made from the waste produced by seat cushion

Promotional gym shoes made for Expo 67 "Man and his world", held in Montreal. These are basically white plimsolls that have a narrow, pointed toe to give them a fashionable look.

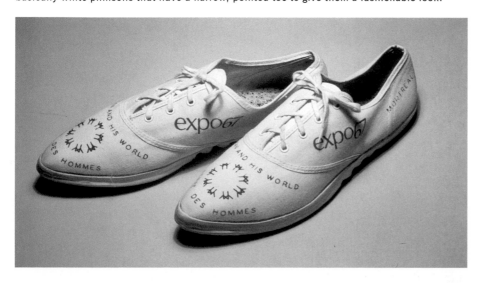

Start-rite

Start-rite shoes have been worn for generations and the company is mentioned in the Guinness Book of Records as the oldest shoemaking company in the world.

Start-rite was founded in the U.K. in1792 by James Smith, a leather merchant. He began producing women's shoes, which were made by people at home in their cottages. In 1816 the firm was taken over by Charles Winter who introduced new American machines for sewing the uppers. In 1856, more machines were imported that attached the uppers to the soles. In 1865, James Southall took over, and it has been in his family's hands ever since.

Until the First World War, the company continued making women's shoes. Soon after, it began making the children's shoes for which it is now famous. By the beginning of the Second World War children's shoes took up half its production, but during the war, this was increased to 83 percent. Since then, Start-rite have concentrated solely on the children's market and many children across the Western world begin their walking life in Start-rite shoes.

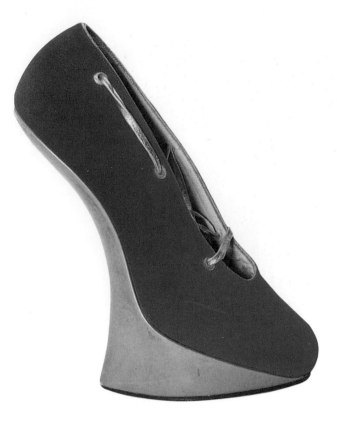

manufacturers. The interfacing between the upper and the inner lining is made from recycled polyester soft drinks bottles. The lining itself is recycled cotton canvas and the heel stiffeners are made from shoe manufacturers' waste trim. Deja Shoe also arranged a system for customers' old Deja shoes to be returned to the company. They are then shredded to make Old Shoe Dog Beds.

Formula One

For years, people in the Third World have been making sandal soles out of old car tyres. In the U.K., Paul Dooner of Dodge Footwear added glamor to recycling and came up with the Formula One range. Dooner bought up used Grande Prix tyres, which are cut up and used as soles for his padded canvas boots.

Health Cults

With the growth of the Green movement in the 1960s, the Birkenstock cult sandal with all its buckles and straps began to sell again. Birkenstocks have been made since 1774, but they became the ultimate anti-fashion statement in 1967, when the Whole-Earth movement began. The Birkenstock has an ergonomically designed insole which mimics the contours of the feet. The wearer's heel fits into a heel cup and the toes are healthily splayed. This idea led to a new health fad in the 1970s.

The Earth Shoe had a sloping sole placing the heel lower than the rest of the foot, which was supposed to equalize the tension in the foot. Although millions were sold in the U.S., the trend for the Earth Shoe was short-lived. The demand for cruelty-free footwear also overwhelmed Vegetarian Shoes. The company began by making a rough-and-ready basketball boot with a car tyre sole, and progressed to making boots and shoes with synthetic uppers.

Dr Scholl, whose wooden sandals were popular in the 1960s and 1970s, also attempted to ride the Green bandwagon back into fashion. Apparently, 95 percent of

Agony to wear, this impossibly balanced court shoe (*above*) was created by André Perugia in the mid 1960s.

The no-heel shoe (*right*). The wearer was supported by the small tongue that extends back from the sole, and the sensation was one of walking on a piece of sprung furniture.

Naked foot sandals (*right*) created by Herbert Levine in 1955. The idea was that the foot would adhere to the pink pads, so the shoe was not visibly secured to the foot.

Another twist on the high heel (*left*). This one is an eyecatching design with a wooden heel.

A gold leather and metal sandal (*below*) with a spring heel, created by the master of handcrafted shoes, André Perugia, in 1962.

Clear vinyl shoes with matching bag, created by Herbert Levine in 1972. The shoes have a silver heel and insole.

Americans still recognize the brand name, and the mid-1990s have seen a slight resurgence of interest among a broader age range.

Shoes that Shock

Shoe designers occasionally produce a shoe that is intended to be a cult object. Some of the weirdest try to make the shoe look like a foot. In 1950, Perugia made his Machine Age pump with a cog-shaped rosette on the front and a heel of twisted steel. He molded toes into the light suede vamp and added toe nails in a darker suede to complete the effect.

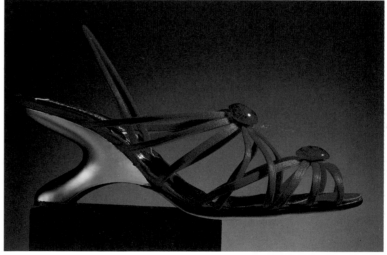

In 1979, shoe designer Andrea Pfister put hands on his feet. He embossed white gloves on shoes in an ironic tribute to jazz singer Al Jolson. Pierre Cardin followed in Perugia's footsteps in 1986 when he made a pair of men's laceup chukkas that were shaped like feet, with the toes and toe nails molded into the leather vamp. The inspiration for these was the 1935 surrealist painting The Red Model by René Magritte, which showed two foot-shaped boots stranded on a beach.

In 1990, Odette Nicoletti molded toes in gold kid on her grosgrain platforms for La Scala's production of the opera Idomeneo. And that same year, the British design group, Lawler Duffy, silkscreened a foot onto a pair of denim chukka boots. In a further surrealist twist, they used the same silk screen for both boots, giving them two left feet.

Early attempts by Ferragamo and others to make "invisible" sandals from Perspex, never really took off. But American shoe designer Beth Levine claims that she had a success with her completely "topless" shoe. It consisted simply of a sole with a high heel. Pads on the insole were soaked in glue and the shoe was stuck to the wearer's foot. Levine even claims to have seen a woman dancing in them.

Christened "Monza" after the Italian motor racing circuit, this is undoubtedly a racy shoe with its cherry red satin straps topped by Venetian glass discs, all set off by a very dynamic, stream-lined heel in matt gold.

133

A CENTURY OF SHOES
1900-2000

Shoes do not exist in isolation. They are part of an overall fashion look, and fashion has changed radically from decade to decade during this century.

Hemlines traveled from below the ankle to the crotch and down again several times. Undergarments used to be something that had to be hidden, but in the late 1990s Wonderbras and big knickers can be seen through diaphanous dresses. Some daring souls have even dispensed with underwear beneath flimsy, seethrough fabrics, a style that would have led to instant arrest in 1900.

During the century, a whole new palette of synthetic colors has been introduced, along with a vast range of new materials and fabrics. Clothes are now made for the masses, rather than the rich few. But those who are wealthy, seek out rare and exotic designers who can create something that will make them stand out from the crowd.

At the beginning of the century, fashion was regimented. There were dress codes to which both men and women conformed. People dressed correctly for each occasion and there was little room for individual expression. The 1990s are more eclectic and people can dress pretty much how they please. There are so many styles to choose from that people are swamped with images and influences from around the world. Fashion shows have become theatrical experiences and showcases for ideas rather than for

Black leather, tongued laceups (*above*) from Joan & David, 1990s, were traditionally for men, but became acceptable wear for both men and women.

Styles came and went through the decades. The ankle-strapped platform sandal (*right*) by Terry de Havilland, 1997 would look fitting on a movie star of the 1930s.

Designs cross-fertilized resulting in innovative combinations. Johnny Moke borrowed classic slingback court shape and "Schiaparelli pink" from the past and added a whacky wooden heel, 1997.

garments which people can actually wear. While some designers look forward to the space age, or the "New Age", or some other utopian future, others rifle the past for inspiration. A style does not have to be out for fashion for more than a few years before it can be reintroduced as "retro". Politics has also invaded clothes. What people wear does not merely say who and what they are, it frequently says what they want to become.

As styles have proliferated and so much media time is given over to dissecting the latest looks, the language of fashion has become more complex. Fashion has become postmodern and wacky combinations of unlikely garments can be put together and outfits worn with irony.

Shoes are an essential part of this postmodern palette: workmen's boots can be worn with a cocktail dress, sneakers with a business suit. Footwear can speak volumes and sneakers, Gucci loafers, stiletto heels, wedges and platform sandals are all redolent of the time in which they were first introduced—and of the times they have become fashionable again. The wearer of a pair of modern shoes carries history on the feet.

Individual expression became increasingly important as international designers vied with each other for supremacy. The shoe (*above*) sets a lightening flash of cerise and purple, on a metal coil heel.

André Pfister takes full advantage of the broad palette of colors that has developed through the decades, in his four-color satin evening mules (*below*).

Color fads change, but black has remained a constant to provide versatility and classic elegance as in Bruno Magli's 1997 evening sandal (*below*).

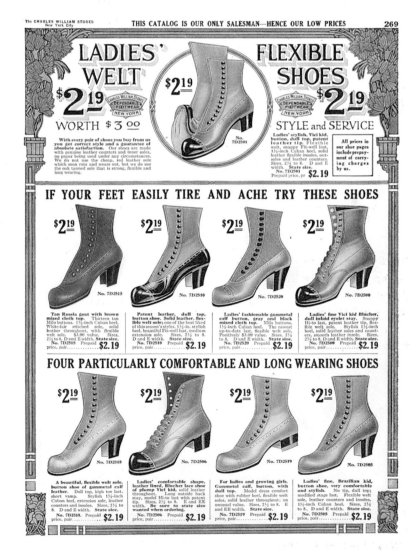

Advertisement (*above*) for ladies' shoes showing that quality, and comfort were important factors when buying shoes in the earlier decades—as was value for money—all at $2.19 a pair, Charles Williams Stores, New York.

The Golden Age

In 1900, most of the high fashions of the century just past were still in vogue. Many stayed in place until the trauma of the First World War.

Skirts were anklelength so women's shoes were seldom seen and tight, buttoned boots were worn outdoors in all seasons. Shoes were selected for cut and quality, rather than style. Black was the color of the 1900s and the use of suede was the only concession to relaxation in the dress code.

Although high button or laced boots remained correct for outdoor wear until the 1920s, laced ankle boots in pale neutrals could be worn in summer from about 1910. Louis, and sloping Cuban heels varied in height from 2—21/2 inches (5—7 cm).

Pumps with small heels came into fashion for daytime wear around 1910. Evening shoes were high cut until 1910 and had straps to hold them in place for dancing. Naked extremities were still considered a little indecent. Boudoir shoes could be more seductive and were made in satin and silk, with tulle bows.

Gradually, these fashions came out of the boudoir on to the street. Evening shoes were decorated with pompoms and bows, and later, with beads or silver chiffon. Even the buckles on

1905

The Becktive "Regal" (*below*), in burgundy kid leather, was popular during the first decade. It combined smartness with comfort, and a low, curved louis heel.

1904

Medium-heeled pumps or court shoes (above) began to be worn instead of the ubiquitous boot that had dominated the late 1800s, as hemlines rose just a little way above the ankle.

walking shoes became larger and bolder and were made of cut or burnished steel. Later, they were seeded with pearls or made of paste, and their shape became more extreme.

The First World War changed everything. Huge numbers of men were drafted into the armed forces and women stepped into their jobs in the factories. Factory work gave some women their own money for the first time and they could choose to spend it on clothes and shoes.

Wartime shortages led to the century's first major shortening of hemlines. Despite the somber mood, shoes became more colorful and silk stockings became more sheer and sexy. The new freedoms the war brought to women meant that their shoes had to be more comfortable and less restricting.

19 OO's

1911

Women in Europe and America were walking more, and street and carriage shoes were developed in a range of widths to maximize individual comfort. Advertisements (*right*) offered practical extras such as "shaped, rubber heels," and suffragettes, in particular, welcomed "sensible" shoes .

1918

Highcut laceup boots, with relatively low heels (*below*), made a comeback during the First World War—a suitable style for active women who had kept men's work going on the home front. There was no shortage of leather as there was to be during the Second World War.

1910

Sand-colored, kid leather, bar strap shoe (*below*) with button trim—the button strap held the shoe in place whilst walking down uneven, cobbled streets during the day—and also for the growing craze for dancing.

The Roaring Twenties

Shoe fashions in the 1920s were exciting and new—with a complete break from the past. New colors and fabrics cascaded onto the market and styles changed radically each season.

In the 1920s, there was an explosion of optimism. World War I was over, the factories were full, and the stock market was climbing. People had money, and they wanted to spend it on clothes. New shoe companies and shoe stores sprang up and machine-made shoes took over from the shoemaker. Fashion was no longer for the elite, stores were full of new styles, and anybody could join in.

Hemlines soared up to the knee—even rising above it in 1927—and people wanted new shoes. The bar shoe with pointed toe and high louis heel is considered the classic shoe of the 1920s. In fact, pumps with tongues, cutaways, T-bars, and crossed straps came into fashion in successive years. Oriental styles were popular in the early 1920s and slides and harem slippers in richly colored brocades appeared.

Shoes had to be sturdy enough to stand up to the dance crazes of the Charleston and the Black Bottom. Then, as dance fever faded later in the decade, shoes become lighter and more

1920

The advertisement reflects a newfound freedom and a zest for the great outdoors following the deprivations of the war years. Many of the clothing and footwear designs of the period forcus on sports and freedom of movement.

1922

Rising hemlines led to a new interest in shoes, and designers began to experiment with fine fabrics, different colors, and intricate leatherwork, as in the selection (*above*) from Clarks, UK. The lively results fitted in with the gaiety of the "Roaring Twenties."

elegant. Heels were high, even for dancing and the Cuban heel came into fashion for walking and sports in 1922. There was an explosion of color: shoes were red, white, and blue leather, and gold kid and gold lamé became fashionable. Evening shoes were made in richly colored velvets and silks smothered with pearls. Beadwork, embossed leather, sequins and embroidered fabrics all had their vogue.

Shoe fashions became so extreme that the foot became the focal point of fashion. By 1925, colors became more muted, and browns, beiges, and grays took over. Art Deco brought in a more geometric look in 1926, but by the end of the decade that too had mellowed.

Buckles started the decade bold and brassy, boasting pearl and rhinestone. From the middle of the decade the buckle declined in importance and, by 1930, it had become very small.

Men's shoes were in similar turmoil. In 1924, the Prince of Wales caused a sensation when he arrived for a tour of the U.S.

wearing suede shoes. These were thought of as caddish. Even brown shoes were seen as somewhat suspect. But by 1925, mens' boots with gray legs were seen. Spectators, in brown and white designs, and then black and white fashionable sports were seen in 1928. By 1929, fashionable men could even be seen wearing blue shoes.

19 20's

1925

The gold kid evening shoe (*right*) has an decorated, inlaid front panel inspired by the mania for Egyptian motifs. Archeologist Howard Carter had opened the sarcophagus of Pharaoh Tutankhamun the previous year.

1929

Bar shoes, with one or more straps across the arch of the foot were the most popular basic style of the decade. Apart from anything else, they stayed on the foot while dancing. The example below is in brocade and gold kid, by Bally of Switzerland.

1926

After the First World War, the economy was booming, people had money to spend, and were in a mood for partying—in shoes like the buckled evening pump in brocade, gold and silver kid (*below*) by Bally of Switzerland.

Seriously Thirty Somethings

By the 1930s, the Great Depression had swept the world. The excesses of the 1920s faded and fashion reflected the new seriousness.

It is said that hemlines rise and fall with the economy. The Wall Street Crash sent daytime hemlines tumbling down to midcalf. Elegance was understated and opulence was out. While the unemployed waited at soup kitchens, no one wanted to look frivolous.

Caught out by the new skirt lengths, Hollywood had to reshoot entire movies to include them. But the 1930s soon proved to be Hollywood's heyday. The talkies had taken over and screen fashions became a more important influence than the couture houses of Paris. Elements of escapism and flights of fantasy crept into everyday fashion.

Comfort became a major consideration for women. The tailored suit was fashionable for women's daywear. To go with it, women needed a more businesslike shoe, so heels became lower, broader and more angular, disappearing altogether on sandals and sports shoes after 1934. Short ankle boots were introduced for outdoor activities. The new fad for the outdoors

1932

A trio of sensible suede "walking" shoes (*right*) by Preciosa for Hérault, of France,were suitably downplayed styles for the economically depressed years of the early 30s. They would have been worn with a tweed suit or tailored dress.

1935

An attempt to capture the style-conscious consumer with a practical item (below). Quarter tips protected heels from wear.

1933

The movie stars of Hollywood, like Leila Hyams, photographed (*left*) at Palm Springs, became role models for the well dressed woman, and were soon exercising more influence on fashion than the haute couture houses of Europe.

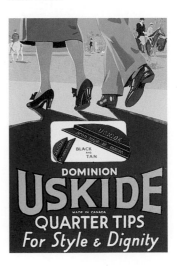

brought sandals to prominence. Starting as beachwear, they developed into partywear and, by the end of the decade, took over as daywear. The style affected court shoes, and open toes and slingbacks were introduced, to instant acclaim.

Sneakers with rubber soles and linen uppers came into fashion and proved hard-wearing. Evening shoes had to be hard-wearing, too. The luxurious silks, satins, and velvets of the beginning of the decade eventually gave way to suede and kid, although exotic hides, such as lizard, remained chic.

Shoes with cork platforms appeared in 1938. The platforms were covered in cloth or leather and decorated with sequins for evening wear. As the decade progressed, gold and silver were discreetly piped on evening shoes. Black was the most popular color for day shoes throughout the decade, but wine, maroon, and navy gradually established a foothold, and pastel colors appeared in 1935. On the eve of the Second World War, there was a sudden explosion of bright colors again.

In the 1930s, boots disappeared from fashionable men's wear. Respectable men wore brogues, while the more raffish wore spectators. The loafer made its first appearance as a fashionable style, and men wore sandals as beachwear and for other outdoor activities.

19 30's

1937
Variations of the T-strap, a perennial favorite of the 20s and 30s. The selection from Dolcis U.K., with cutaway swides and open toes reflects the influence of the sandal on classic shoe shapes.

1939
Twotone brogues, known as "spectators" in the U.S. and "co-respondents" in the U.K., reached the height of their popularity in the 1930s. The fact that they were a favorite style of tapdancing movie star Fred Astaire may have contributed to this.

A New Look

The 1940s were dominated by the war—there were shortages of materials and fashions were regulated by statute. In 1947, Dior's New Look turned the world of fashion on its head.

After the Japanese attack on Pearl Harbor, the king of luxury fashion, Stanley Marcus was summoned to the White House. His job, President Roosevelt said, was to sell wartime clothing restrictions to the American people.

The U.S. government conserved leather and limited shoes to six colors. The maximum height of heels was fixed at 1 inch (2.5 cm) and American women were urged to buy comfortable wedges or low heels, so they could walk further and save gasoline. There was rationing in Britain too, but British women were allowed heels up to 2 inches (5 cm).

As apparel consultant to the War Production Board, Stanley Marcus told the fashion industry to promote styles that would remain in fashion, releasing factory space and labor for war work. Shoppers were advised to buy only high quality merchandise that would last the duration of the war.

The corksoled, covered platform and the wedge, introduced

1944

In the U.S. concessions were made to heat and fashion, as in the crocodile opentoed slingbacks (*left*). They would probably have been paired with a matching bag.

1942

The first wedge heels appear during the war years. The Italian designer Ferragamo was said to have introduced a cork version when he was experimenting with alternative materials. The chisel-toed pair below, though, with minimal punched decoration, are English.

1940

The women's armed forces set the tone for wartime footwear: strictly no-nonsense laceups or strap and buckle shoes. There was a shortage of leather and clothes were rationed. Shoes were made to last.

in Europe, had already come into style in the U.S. in the late 1930s. However, to save materials in wartime, the platform and the wedge were stripped of their covering, leaving the cork exposed.

With the Paris couture houses behind enemy lines, young American designers came into their own. In 1944, Claire McCardell commissioned the New York ballet slipper firm Capezio to make a rugged version for outdoors wear. It was a shrewd creation because ballet slippers fell outside U.S. wartime restrictions.

College students began wearing sports clothes. Initially, they adopted a British look and wore spectator pumps and saddle shoes, but more casual styles came from Texas and the West Coast. In Harlem and other black ghettos young blacks and Hispanics developed long, pointed shoes that later became known as winklepickers.

After the war many restrictions stayed in force. In 1947, the designer Christian Dior opened a couture house in Paris. He dropped hemlines to just above the ankle and introduced a full, pleated skirt with voluminous petticoats. The authorities were shocked, but women in Europe and America were converted almost overnight. However, clumpy platform shoes and wedges were out of place with the New Look and were replaced with slimsoled court shoes and sandals.

19 40's

1948
Shoes to go with the new, postwar tailored dress (*right*) which was popular for afternoon wear. Everyone wore a hat, and the most stylish would carry a fur stole.

1946
Still clumpy and practical as a hangover from the war, but these twotone laceups (below), by Bally of Switzerland, display an almost frivolous, immaculate attention to detail.

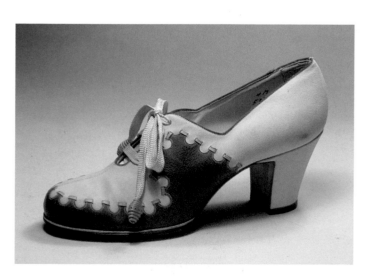

The Wild Ones

The 1950s began with Christian Dior's New Look and ended with rock and roll. The decade also managed to embrace both stilettos and sneakers.

Dior's New Look brought the fashion world back to Paris, but the Italians were a formidable force in shoe fashion. In Italy's postwar boom their shoe factories made many technical and design changes. The light, elegant Italian sandal became their most distinctive export and the race to slim down the heel was on.

Who first created the stiletto heel is still open to argument. In France, Charles Jourdan paved the way with a steel and wood heel in 1951. Italian shoe manufacturers called their new narrow heels stilettos in 1953. But Roger Vivier, Dior's shoe designer, is credited with making the first true stiletto in 1955. After that, stiletto heels appeared on court shoes and pumps, and stiletto heels kept rising until the fashion peaked in about 1958.

Givenchy and Chanel had fought the stiletto since 1955 and both designed a lower pump. In 1958, Dior made other innovations and introduced a T-strap and a wedge toe to his shoes.

1950

The advent of the inoffensive desert boot (*right*)—more of a shoe which nudged the ankle bone—marked one of the first, cult shoes of the young generation. It was a soft suede version of the polo chukka boot, with two eyelets.

1955

Sandals had arrived from Italy. Many were extremely elegant, but there were also the first opentoed sandals that molded "ergonomically" around the sole of the foot (*below*), which were bestsellers in the 1950s.

1951

Velvet, preferably black, was a popular party option, especially if you could manage matching gloves, bag, and shoes (*left*). The court shoe with the cutaway sides became popular, and with its sturdy heel, went a treat with the fuller skirts that were still celebrating the postwar years.

Roger Vivier made the gold kidskin shoes studded with rubies that Queen Elizabeth II wore at her coronation in 1953. This sort of opulence had not been seen since the 1920s. A craze for richly adorned Turkish slippers followed. Court shoes in watered silk became fashionable for evening wear and pumps sported large bows.

During the 1950s Dior reestablished the power of the haute couture houses and the rich flocked to Paris for the collections. The French shoe manufacturer Charles Jourdan cashed in by opening a boutique in Paris. In response, Italian manufacturers organized shoe fairs and competitions to lure rich customers south.

In America, the "preppy" look arrived. Loafers spread outside the colleges and were taken up by the young. Then a more rebellious look came in: teenage girls wore colored sneakers with their white bobby sox and teenage boys turned to All Star basketball boots. British youth adopted the winklepicker, while the desert boot was launched on the civilian population. These boots had little appeal for rebellious youth, so Teddy boys wore brothel creepers, which had thick crepe soles and lurid suede uppers. These youth fashions seemed marginal at first, but as the postwar baby boomers grew up, they took over the fashion world and in 1956, Mary Quant opened her first boutique in London's Kings Road.

19 50's

1956

Black suede court shoe with punched decoration (*left*) and a low platform. By this time, the mania for sandals had virtually made platforms obsolete.

Made by **JOHN WHITE**
AS SHEWN ON
TV

WITH *PLEXOR* Soles

3 TIMES THE LIFE OF LEATHER

49/9

1957

The "we've never had it so good" era described by U.K. Prime Minister Harold Macmillan was pretty universal in the western world and reflected in such fripperies as the U.S. cabinet slide (*right*), and the stiletto heel.

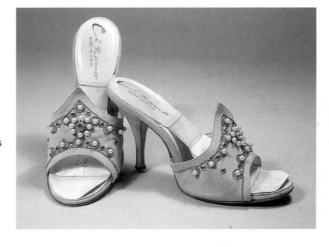

1959

Until now, leather soles were the norm. But in the late 50s, new materials were on their way, such as the Plexor sole advertised (*above*).

Street Scene

In the 1960s, the center of the fashion world moved from Paris to London, and it was the new street style, rather than haute couture, that led fashion.

"Couture is for grannies," declared the French actress Brigitte Bardot in the early 60s. Yves Saint Laurent outraged his traditional customers with his street style and ready-to-wear boutique, Rive Gauche. There was a general reaction against the middleclass values of the postwar years, and young designers, such as Mary Quant in London, tried to keep up with the fast-changing whims of the new youth culture. Fashion was made by the customer, not the couturier, and the chain stores looked to Mary Quant, rather than French couture houses to show them the fashion trends. Fashion no longer belonged to movie stars and socialites; everyone was involved and the leaders of the new youth fashions were the new super pop stars. The Beatles popularized the elastic-sided Chelsea boot and, later, the Beatle boot, with its side zipper and Cuban heel. Colored suedes were popular for men's shoes. Women went for a schoolgirl look with lowheeled pumps and bar shoes, and wore them with long white socks.

1961

The steel pin introduced in the 1950s took shoe design to new heights. The rising youth culture might have been in pumps, but their elegant elders were firmly in stilettos, largely led by the Italian designers such as Ferragamo and Perugia, although the example above is by Bally, inspired by Gobelin tapestry.

1962

After the 1960s movie *La Dolce Vita*, featuring the actress Anita Ekberg paddling in Rome's Trevi fountain, stilettos in hand, high heels were not completely threatened. The shoes had starring roles in the movies *Catwoman* and *Barbarella* too. Here's a Bruno Magli, very Italian design: understated and elegant with a tiny buckle and punched topline.

1965

Pants (trousers) became acceptable wear for women for both formal and casual wear in the 60s, and slipon shoes like the Bruno Magli pump with buckle (*above*) were ideal accompaniments. The shiny "wetlook" finish was another new trend.

The Parisian designers were not totally outflanked. The most copied shoe of the time was Roger Vivier's Pilgrim pump with silver buckles. When leather prices rose manufacturers took to wetlook vinyls and other synthetics—for jackets and coats as well as shoes and bags. Vivier, Herbert Levine and I. Miller pioneered clear plastic, while Yves Saint Laurent popularized mock croc. The popular Space Age look was achieved with silver finishes, and patent leather appeared in strong colors.

André Courrèges introduced flat, shiny white boots with square toes in his 1964 Space Age collection. Mary Quant followed suit, although hers were made in injection-molded plastic. Vivier saw which way things were going and produced thigh boots in crocodile for Yves Saint Laurent.

Kneelength boots were teamed with miniskirts, and as the 1960s progressed, loose boots with a front seam gave way to boots that clung more tightly to the leg. Treated leathers and textiles took over from plain leather and plastic.

After 1967, an ethnic look came in. Strappy African and oriental sandals were worn with flowing robes, afghan coats, and cheesecloth skirts and blouses. Pumps were abandoned in favor of more solid shoes, with broad, square heels. Soles thickened too, paving the way for the comeback of platforms.

19 60's

1966
Miniskirts revealed large expanses of leg, and the opportunity to show off some zany boot designs such as the printed fake zebra fur pair from the U.S. (*left*).

1965
It was a time of flicked and backcombed hairstyles, and leggy models. Coco Chanel's *mannequins* (*below*) are wearing the enduring twotone slingback court shoe which Chanel had introduced in the previous decade.

1969
Soles thickened towards the end of the decade, paving the way for the platform (*below*). Paloma Picasso claimed to have designed the first of the new wave platforms, in 1968. The style reached London's trendsetting Biba boutiques the same year and sold more than 75,000 pairs in a couple of months.

The Glam Era

The 1970s world of fashion will always be remembered for the androgynous styles of "glam" rock and outrageous platform boots.

The 70s were also the years in which minority groups, including women, gay men and lesbians, and ethnic communities, made their presence felt and contributed to the cultural and style scene. The result was a melting pot of fashion, although couture houses continued to produce classics, with the emphasis on elegance and wearability.

In London, platforms were popularized by Barbara Hulanicki, who owned the ultra-fashionable Biba store, and trendy designer Terry de Havilland. Rock stars such as David Bowie and Gary Glitter tottered on stage wearing 6 or 7 inch (15—17.5 cm) silver stacks. Platform boots were popular for both women and men. In Italy shoe manufacturers readied themselves to swamp the mass market.

To complement a fashion for the briefest of hotpants, women's boots reached the thigh. Color was important and boots were painted with psychedelic designs and appliquéd with

1972

Exciting textures and patterns were all part of the glamorous side of the 70s scene, as in the heavily embroidered, "wetlook", fitted Canadian boots (*below*). Favorite colors were black, white, and red.

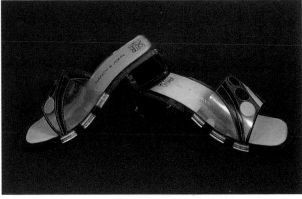

1974

Designers experimented with new materials, and trying to achieve the lightest of shoes, like the clear Perspex and plastic slipons (*above*).

1975

Fashion was branching in two contrasting directions by the mid 70s: one was the sensible route, typified by the conventional tie shoes (*below*). They are given an uplift by the wooden clog-style sole and are said to have been worn by the rock musician Elton John.

suede flowers and fruits. Patchwork boots of clashing colors were also fashionable. Texture was an important feature, and included tapestry, printed burlap, suede, linen, distressed canvas, and wet-look surfaces.

By the mid-1970s, the oil crisis had led to a world economic depression, and a more conservative, businesslike look took over. There was a definite preference for clothes fashions that would last for more than a season. Women, many more of whom were going out to work, wore low pumps with a single strap and cowboy boots in black leather. In the evening, they wore unadorned pumps, slingbacks, and simple sandals.

Men wore tasseled or buckled loafers, and motorcycle and army-style boots.

But fashion was becoming more segmented with different groups reacting to different trends. By 1977, many of the young turned to punk and dressed to offend. Clothes were slashed or covered with obscene images and aggressive slogas.Vivienne

Westwood produced bondage boots covered in straps and buckles. Clothes and shoes sprouted functionless zippers. The Dr. Marten boot began its relentless rise as the symbol of urban rebellion. Those worn by skinheads sported steel toe caps, while punks painted them lurid colors.

But mainstream fashion turned its back on street styles. The affluent turned to the classics and to the young, ready-to-wear designers who were flocking to Paris and New York.

the 19 70's

1976

A nostalgic look back to the past for inspiration was a feature of the mid 70s. The "retro-chic" opentoed platform shoes (above), are reminiscent of 40s glamour.

1976

A new wave of designers was exploring the full potential of shoe structure. The Dutchman Jan Jansen, responsible for the high wooden platform shoes (below), with a definite hippy look to the raw edge suede upper.

1976

Plastic shoes in every shape and form hit the scene, including the almost invisible "Exorcist" brand (above) made in Mexico for the Canadian market.

Designer Labels

The 1980s was the decade of the designer and the most important fashion accessory was a designer label.

I t was vital to dress for success in the 1980s. In the full flowering of designer labels, Armani made the suits and Gucci the loafers, handbags and other accessories. The designer label began in the 1960s, when Pierre Cardin oversold his franchise. Next in the label game was Halston, who made his name through Jacqueline Kennedy's pillbox hats. Norton Simmon Inc. purchased the right to franchise Halston's name in 1973. By the 1980s, the Hong Kong jeans manufacturer Murjani had persuaded New York socialite Gloria Vanderbilt to put her signature on its jeans and be photographed in them. The effect was instantaneous, in the first year, sales multiplied sixfold.

It was all part of the revolution in fashion retailing. The big fashion houses could no longer depend on creating for an exclusive private clientele—that market was diminishing. They had to diversify into ready-to-wear, accessories, licensing and franchising, to meet the needs of a more general market. In the

1980

The ankle boot (*right*), once a traditional parter for full-length skirts or pants (trousers), were now designed to accompany shorter styles.

1981

Designers began to fudge the boundaries between one type of shoe and another. Just short of the ankle boot is a highcut, beautifully sculptured, asymmetrical, shoe (*below*) in maroon suede with discreet embroidery, by Georgis Moretti, Canada.

1980

Designers began to fudge the boundaries between one type of shoe and another. Just short of the ankle boot is a highcut, beautifully sculptured, asymmetrical, shoe (*left*) in maroon suede with discreet embroidery, by Georgis Moretti, Canada.

1980s, the big French shoe manufacturer Charles Jourdan, and the top Italian manufacturers flocked to sell their styles and their names through the big American department stores. Here there was a growing trend for stores within stores, which were arranged by designer.

The shoe of the decade was the plain black pump, which was sometimes decorated with a buckle. As the decade wore on, colors, though muted at first, began to reappear. Bows and rosettes of chiffon blossomed on court shoes and slowly and discreetly designers began to stud the heels of evening shoes with jewels.

Although 1980s "yuppies" (the Young, Upwardly Mobile set) were living it up by night, they were getting fit by day. Jogging and going to the gym became fashionable, and the tennis or training shoe became ubiquitous. As with 1980s clothes, the name on the tennis shoe was all important. It had to be Reebok, Nike, Fila, Adidas, or Puma. Young rappers took to tennis shoes as dance shoes. The rap-crossover band Run DMC had a hit with a track called My Adidas in 1987. Some teenagers kept collections of 20 or 30 pairs of the big-name styles. However, when Pierre Cardin, or other non sports names, appeared on tennis shoes it did not work. They had to be Nike, Air Jordans *et al*, or nothing.

19 80's

1986

Dr Martens boots were the uniform of the anti-fashion punk scene (*left*), but they gradually lost their wild image and became acceptable streetwear for a wider, more respectable, but still fashion-conscious youth market.

1985

The classic Chanel twotone slingback court kept coming back (*below*). It was ideally suited to the new wave of professional women and the booming businesses of the early 80s. Seven different variations of the shoe are offered each season.

1989

Manufacturers of sports shoes (*right*) were outdoing each other in the latest hightech specifications for their products. The technology is important, but the right designer label is crucial for street credibility.

Back to the Future

By the 1990s, it seemed as if designers simply recycled ideas from earlier decades, turning retro into a fashion in its own right.

In the 1990s any fashion of the postwar era could be revisited, plundered and served up again, only this time it had to be more extreme. Vivienne Westwood and Jean-Paul Gaultier brought back the platform shoe yet again. Vivienne Westwood explored retro further than other designers, going back into the bustiers and corsets of previous centuries. In general, women could select from an eclectic range of styles to suit every mood, business, or social occasion. Comfortable, lowheeled walking shoes, high stilettos, and midheight heels were executed in a variety of leathers, suedes and fabrics.

The name was all. Brand names such as Gucci, Louis Vuitton, Escada, Donna Karan, Moschino, Versace, and Pollini were seen as very desirable, and it was essential to wear sport-inspired shoes by Timberland, CATS, Campers, and Big Rigg, among others. Established names such as Kickers took on young designers, and Nike, Fila, Reebok, and Adidas continued to offer exciting and imaginative new concepts.

1992

The decade seemed to have difficulty in finding a strong new direction of its own, so it looked into the past. It's back to the 60s (*below*), with the reintroduced Chelsea boot.

1990

Tennis or training shoes (*above*) become increasingly flash, hightech, and sculptural, and are now worn not only in the gym, but in the street, and for clubbing.

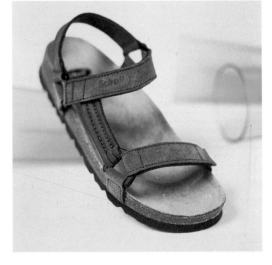

1993

Back to "Nature"—the name for the healthy ergonomically designed sandal (*above*). It is a Birkenstock original, and like every other design, launched a thousand copies in an age when sensible sandals were suddenly acceptable again.

The 1990s saw the rise of the couturier shoe designer, and Manolo Blahnik is unquestionably the star. Madonna said of Blahnik: "His shoes are wonderful, and they last longer than sex." Many of this new generation of shoe designers work out of London.

Technology has had a huge impact. Materials such as microfibers, stretch fabrics and various synthetic materials are used to great effect. Technology has also improved the manufacturing process, and computerized embroidery and other new methods of decoration have brought elaborate designs to the mass market. The Far East has risen as a major mass producer of shoes.

There has been some nostalgia too. The 1970s revival spawned platforms, stilettos, strippy sandals, and high boots, while names such as Birkenstock sandals, Hush Puppies and desert boots, once derided by the young, began to be reviewed as the ultimate in trendy footwear.

Ecology was an important theme and there are those who wanted to get out into the environment or, at the very least, look as if they did. Timberland and Rockport boots were for them. They are the tough styles of the great American outdoors, now familiar on the streets and the campuses of the U.S. and Europe.

19 90's

1995

By the middle of the decade, the 90s were finally asserting a style of their own. The fashion shoe (*above*) combines the sports shoe concept with a definitely unsporty platform and heel.

1996

Dr Martens made the move from fringe punk "bovver" boots to popular accessories with smart clothes (*right*).

1997

Strappy sandals make a sensational comeback (*above and right*), this time with innovative twists to the styles as in this collection by Prada, which established itself as a leading trendsetter of the decade.

2001. A Shoe Odyssey

A glimpse into the future is provided by students at Cordwainer's College in London, where many of today's top designers trained.

When Manolo Blahnik was asked what shoes will be worn after the Millennium, he said: "A good hat, a good pair of shoes, a good dress will always be a good hat, a good pair of shoes, a good dress. People will insist on quality, quality, quality. We will get rid of trash and get back to good things."

At all levels in the market, people like brand and designer names on their shoes, and designer label shoemakers such as Blahnik will certainly still be very much in vogue after the year 2000.

During the current century clothes have become increasingly casual. Even the modern business suit is a far less constricting item of clothing than its predecessors. As part of this relaxation process, items of sportswear have frequently come into wider use. The sneaker (or trainer) that is now worn on the street evolved from shoes designed for specific sports, such as athletics, soccer, or basketball.

As leisure time increases, and sport options become more diverse, sports shoes in and out of the sporting arenas, are here

Contemporary architecture was the inspiration for this cleancut, seductive shoe by Behnaz Kanani (*left*).

Joanna Whitehead's striking curved wedge heel is combined with "flower fairy" colors of periwinkle blue and lavender studded with bugle beads (*below*).

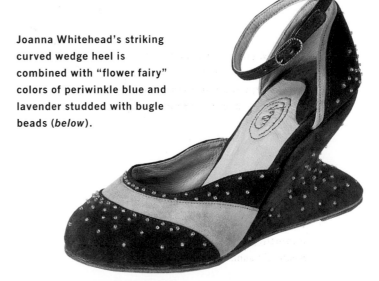

New way of fastening: Rachel Innes' uses metalized fabric which scrunches together to fasten the shoe (*below*).

Suede combines with fabric in these snazzy but practical laceups with Batman mask tabs, by Masahiro Wakabayashi (*below*).

to stay, making further inroads into the fashion scene by transmuting into "athleisure" shoes—that is, athletics shoes used for streetwear. Alternative, mountainbased sports such as trail running, scrambling, and mountain biking brought with them "approach" shoes, which are a cross between traditional hiking boots and high performance sports shoes. They have light, flexible uppers with mesh panels to let the foot breathe, intricate lacing systems, and highly contoured soles..

The development of highly specialized shoes for new sports has encouraged the development of new materials, new features, and new methods of construction which has spilled over into every area of shoe design.The trend for sportswear developed partly because people began to identify more strongly with outdoor lifestyles. But the modern shoe buyer is also passionate about technology. Sales staff have to go on special courses with the manufacturers so that they can satisfy the buyer's thirst for technical specifications.

Increasing concern about the environment has also had an ongoing effect on foot fashion, with more and more pressure on manufacturers to use eco-friendly materials and energy-efficient methods. The swelling ranks of vegetarians are seeking alternatives to leather shoes.

Tougher, more hardwearing materials, including new forms of carbon, are being developed, with waterproofing and stain resistance as priorities, whether shoes are in natural or manmade materials. Increasing computerization in manufacturing techniques will result in the growth of customization of massmarket shoes. A laser scan of a customer's feet could be fed directly to manufacturing machines, which would then produce shoes to a client's exact specifications. Style, color, and trimmings could also be keyed in.

With the availability of new advances in technology, exciting material developments, the disappearance of conventional fashion barriers, and a global marketplace, the future looks set for imaginative and original concepts. As the founder of Ecco, Karl Toonsbury, says: "We are standing on a springboard, with the best possible takeoff into the future. Ahead of us are great challenges. The greatest and most exciting ever."

A classic and comfortable mule by Betty Almond in a brilliant blue-dyed fabric shot with silver cotton mesh (*right*).

Even the soles can be interesting as in Betty Almond's sandals (*below*).

Angela Marti's velvet and wood sandals are inspired by Japanese art and calligraphy (*below*).

Index

Credits

Quarto would like to thank all the following for providing pictures used in this book. While every effort has been made to acknowledge all copyright holders we would like to apologize should there have been any omissions.

Key: t=top b=below c=centre l=left r=right

Adidas (U.K) Ltd p.126(tr); Andrea Pfister p.18/19, p.27, p.34(t), p.37, p.51, p.61(tl), p.70(bl), p.71(t), p.88(t), p.110(r), p.133(b), p.135(cl); Andrea Pfister/Courtesy of the Museum at the F.I.T. New York p.1; Avertising Archive p.97(t), p.129(bl); Agent Provocateur p.35(c); AMF Bowling Inc. U.K p.124(bl); Angela Marti p.155(br); The Bally Shoe Museum p.6, p.15(tl&tr), p.17(br), p.35(b), p.52, p.57(l), p.59(b), p.62, p.87(br), p.94, p.98(br), p.99(t), p.111(b), p.114(tl), p.115(c&b), p.136(b), p.139, p.141(br), p.144(br), p.146(tl); The Bata Shoe Museum p.7(tl&tr), p.8, p.12, p.14(t), p.14(bl), p.15(b), p.16, p.17(t, cr&bl), p.20, p.21(t&bl), p.24, p.25(tr), p.26, p.28, p.29, p.32(t), p.33(t), p.33(cl&bl), p.34(b), p.35(tr), p.36, p.38(b&r), p.39, p.41(t), p.42(bl&tr), p.43(t&b), p.44, p.45, p.46, p.47(t), p.47(bl&br), p.53(cr&br), p.56(cr&bl), p.59(tl), p.60(bl, bc&br), p.61(bl&bc), p.64(b), p.65(t), p.66, p.70(t&br), p.71(cl), p.72, p.74, p.75, p.78, p.80, p.81(tl&bl)(cr&br), p.84, p.87(t&bl), p.88(b&c), p.90(t&br), p.91(b), p.99(br), p.104, p.106(b), p.111(t&c), p.112, p.113, p.116(tl&tr), p.117, p.122, p.128, p.129(tl), p.130(t), p.131(t&b), p.132(cl&cr), p.133(t), p.136(t), p.140(t), p.142(tc&br), p.143(l), p.145(b), p.147(t&br), p.148, p.149(tr), p.150(tl&b); Behnaz Kanani Leather p.154(tl); Birkenstock p.63, p.71(bl&br), p.130(cl); Betty Almond p.155(t&bl); The Boot Store p.116(bl); British Olympic Association p.125(b); Bruno Magli p.11(tl), p.21(cr&br), p.115(tr), p.120(tl), p.121(br&c), p.135(bl), p.146(tr&b); Capital Pictures p.76; Catherine Edwards p.73, p.83(bl&bc); Catskill Mountain Moccasins p.102(tl&bl); Caterpiller Inc.p.105; Chanel p.147(bl),p.151(bl),p.153(br); The Charles Jourdan Museum 'Romans' p.40, p.41(c&b), p.42(tl), p.48(t), p.56(tl), p.59(tr), p.61(tr&br), p.64(l), p.67(b), p.132(tl&br); The Charles William Stores NYC p.14(br), p.86(b), p.107,p.135(br); Christie's Images p.10, p.50; Churches p.91(t); Clarks Shoes p.9(b), p.129(tr), p.138(r), p.144(t); Converse All Star p.124(tl), p.124(br), p.125(tr), Corbis Bettman/UPI p.43(r), p.106(t), p.137(br), p.140(bl), p.142(tl); Cordwainers College p.137(bl), p.145(tl), p.149(tl); Diesel p.130(bl);

DKNY p.83(tr), p.123, p.130(cr); Dr. Martens Air Wair Ltd p.118, p.119, p.151(t), p.153(bl); Dooney & Bourke p.103(tl), p.121(cr); Dunlop p.126(tl); Emma Hope Shoes p.23, p.102(tr); Et Archive p.7(b), p.65(b); Fila (U.K) Ltd p.126(b), p.127(t); Freed of London Ltd p.32(b); Gamba Time Step p.144(bl); G.H. Bass & Co. p.98(t); Gucci p.11(b), p.90(bl), p.120(bl); Hush Puppies UK Ltd p.103(bc&br), p.129(br);
Jan Jansen p.81(tr), p.82, p.149(b), p.150(tr); Jimmy Choo p.49, p.60(tl); Joan & David p.22, p.33(cr), p.48(c&b), p.91(c), p.103(tr), p.120(br), p.121(tl), p.134(tl); Johanna Innes p.154(tr); Johnny Moke p.13, p.134(br), p.132(bl); Johnston & Murphy p.9(t), p.92, p.93; Joseph Azagury p.54, p.55; Katherine Hamnett p.25, p.102(cr), p.103(bl); Loake p.97(b), p.152(b); Lobb of St James p.85, p.89; Manolo Blahnik p.30, p.31; Masahiro Wakabayashi Leather p.11(tc); Nike (UK) Ltd p.125(tl), p.151(br); Patrick Cox p.100, p.101; Prada p.58, p.83(br), p.153(tr); Puma UK p.127(b), p.152(tl), p.153(tl); Rachel Innes p.11(tr), p.154(bl); Red or Dead Ltd p.71(cr); Robert Clergerie p.67(c); Robert Opie Collection p.38(t), p.131(tr), p.137(t), p.138(l), p.140(br), p.141(t), p.143(r), p.145(tr); R-Soles p.108, p.109, p.110(l); Salvatorre Ferragamo p.24(tl), p.68, p.69, p.77(t), p.114(c&b); Scholl p.130(br), p.152(tr); Sebago Inc. p.95, p.98(bl), p.99(bl); Sperry Top Sider p.96(l&r); Ta Ta/Jive Pace p.83(tl); Terry De Havilland/The Magic Shoe Co. p.79, p.121(tr&cl), p.134(bl), p.135(tr); Timberland (UK) Ltd p.116(br); UFAC p.47(r); Visual Arts Library p.57(r);